THE LITTLE ENCYCLOPEDIA
OF JEWISH CULTURE

THE LITTLE ENCYCLOPEDIA

OF Jewish

Culture

101 People, Places, Things (and Foods) Every Jew Should Know

Mathew Klickstein

ROCKRIDGE PRESS

First Rockridge Press trade paperback edition 2022

Rockridge Press and the Rockridge Press logo are trademarks or registered trademarks of Callisto Media Inc. and/or its affiliates in the United States and other countries and may not be used without written permission.

For general information on our other products and services, please contact our Customer Care Department within the United States at (866) 744-2665, or outside the United States at (510) 253-0500.

Paperback ISBN: 979-8-88608-108-4 | eBook ISBN: 979-8-88608-870-0

Manufactured in the United States of America

Interior and Cover Designers: Jamison Spittler and Heather Krakora
Art Producer: Cristina Coppin
Editor: Alexis Sattler
Production Editor: Ashley Polikoff
Production Manager: Riley Hoffman

Ilustrations © 2022 Leia Kaprov; All other illustrations used under license from Shutterstock.com

10 9 8 7 6 5 4 3 2 1 0

*In memory of Todd Gitlin
(January 6, 1943–February 5, 2022)
Activist, Writer, Cultural Critic,
Scholar, Friend, Cousin*

INTRODUCTION

Shalom (or welcome), dear reader! This book, a celebration of Jewish culture, is written for you, whoever you may be, whether you identify as culturally or religiously Jewish, or don't identify as Jewish at all.

As to whom it was written *by*, well . . . I was that kid who, when asked to portray a hero onstage as part of a sixth grade project, chose to be . . . *George Burns*. In *1992*. My middle-school hero was a nonagenarian comedian, and I was proud of it.

To be fair, by that point I was already notorious for bucking contemporary trends. In third grade, our school librarian had called in my mother to report her concern that I was checking out *far* too many books on classic movie monsters from the 1930s to the 1950s.

What I'm getting at is that I don't remember a time in my life when I *wasn't* working toward becoming what some might refer to as a "pop culture historian." During my two-decade career, most of my books, articles, and documentaries have focused on pop culture history. In fact, during the last few weeks of penning the pages that lie before you, I learned that my book on the early years of Nickelodeon, *SLIMED!*, was featured as a clue on *Jeopardy!*

Since I also enjoy working with children on developing their own original theater shows and short film projects, I've recently spent a lot of creative brainstorming time with the next generation. Now, these kids are always great. But I've been disheartened by how few have been introduced to the Three Stooges, the Marx Brothers, and even key cultural shibboleths like "slapstick," "vaudeville," and the "Borscht Belt." All things that are not only very important to me but to my cultural heritage as a Jew, as well.

It got me worried. "If these kids don't know the simple pleasures of watching a good black-and-white cream pie fight on-screen, what future does humanity really have?"

Combine this concern with what I've seen as the diminishment of a substantial cultural legacy in the long-standing tradition of Judaism to cherish and delight in the intersection of our community, our history, and our heritage *with* that wider collective culture writ large.

To have the opportunity now to engage my professional skills as a pop culture historian (whatever the heck *that* means) while zeroing in on cultural elements of being a contemporary Jew today (whatever the heck *that* means) is something for which I'm extremely grateful. Know that the entries in this book are just a few of those I hope I can illuminate for the extant generations and for those to come.

Thanks for stopping in for a look, and I hope you learn something new. Like the fact that current Jewish *Jeopardy!* host Mayim Bialik is an *actual* neuroscientist like her character Dr. Amy Farrah Fowler on *The Big Bang Theory*. Or that George Burns was *eighty* when he accepted his Academy Award . . . and continued to keep us all laughing for another two decades.

Or that such people ever existed in the first place.

HOW TO USE THIS BOOK

I did what I could to keep this book accessible, fast-moving, and—dare I aspire—lighthearted. It was my goal to create something referencing both old and new Jewish icons, along with a range of subjects that go from quite familiar to quite obscure and "niche." I also opened up a fairly large space around the idea of who and what counts as Jewish, rather than abiding by an oft-cited practice of using maternal heritage or including only subjects who consider themselves Jewish by birth or practice.

Each of the 101 blurb-like entries includes a few introductory notes, followed by an explanatory description, footnotes, and finally some suggestions on where you can learn more about the subject.

These entries are interspersed (alphabetically, of course) with fifteen spreads targeting larger categories—Jewish delis, Jewish philosophers, commonly used Yiddish words, etc.

Although this book is certainly one you can read from cover to cover, it can also be used as a quick flip-through reference guide; hence the index and resources in the back pages.

Ultimately, this is a book whose central conceit is one of *sharing* and *conversation*. Sharing of information about the complex and beautiful intricacies of Jewish culture over the past three thousand years . . . along with a few laughs and maybe even a little insight.

Adam Sandler's "The Chanukah Song"

- Uplifting novelty song that embraces a litany of Jewish celebrities, co-written and performed by Jewish comedy icon Adam Sandler
- First performed on *Saturday Night Live*'s "Weekend Update," December 3, 1994
- Sandler has gone on to create three updated versions, altogether roll-calling nearly ninety famous Jews[1]

A generation of Jewish comedy fans coming up in the 1980s and '90s intimately bonded over Adam Sandler's early routines as a unique beacon of modern-day Jewish humor. Sandler made his way onto playlists bumping in cabins and cafeterias at Jewish summer camps around the country well before the rest of the world caught on to his genius. It was therefore of little surprise but much *kvelling*[2] when the budding comic's song about both Chanukah and famous Jews helped launch him into a whole new echelon of mainstream success that continues to this day.

LEARN MORE: Aside from Sandler's own updates to the song over the years, there have been multiple covers, parodies, and alternative versions by amateur and professional musicians alike. Jewish sister rocker trio HAIM performed their spin on the song for *SNL* on the same set where Sandler had played the original . . . twenty-seven years to the day earlier.

---

1   Some of whom, like the Three Stooges and Beastie Boys, were grouped together . . . and some of whom, like Courtney Love and baseball Hall of Famer Rod Carew, were misidentified (though, at least Carew found the misunderstanding amusing)
2   Sense of immense pride

All the Schmooze That's Fit to Print

Whether as "language" or "dialect," Yiddish remains a *mameloshn* or "mother tongue" of Jews. Even if—let's be honest—a striking number of Jews today couldn't point to their own *pupik*.[3] There are fairly common words like *schmutz* (dirt) or *verklempt* (overcome) out there. But for the most part, attempting Yiddish can these days make someone feel like a real schlemiel.[4]

Literally meaning "Jewish," Yiddish's exact provenance is impossible to pinpoint. Aside from Yiddish originating a *very* long time ago, Judaism itself was long an *oral* tradition. The oldest sentence printed in Yiddish appeared three hundred years after it was first spoken. It took an *additional* three hundred years before the Hebrew author and grammarian Élie Lévita produced the first Yiddish dictionary in 1542.

The accepted theory is that Yiddish spouted from the mouths of tenth-century Eastern and Central European (aka Ashkenazi) Jews as a mishmash of predominantly Hebrew, Aramaic, and German words, peppered with those from Slavic and Romantic languages for good measure.

This consommé of ingredients is not too dissimilar from the endonymic jargon spoken by the primary characters in Anthony Burgess's novel *A Clockwork Orange*. Here the characters speak a futuristic slang that integrates combined elements of Russian, Polish, and German. It's a cryptic code

3 Belly button
4 Buffoon

the boys use to keep secrets hidden from outsiders. Yiddish was similarly used in European Jewish ghettos during World War II, so that Jews could converse safely without fear of being understood by their Nazi gauleiters.

According to calculations by Rutgers University, Yiddish is spoken by less than 4 percent of the approximately 15.2 million Jews alive today. On the upside, there continue to be those who passionately keep Yiddish alive by speaking it, analyzing it, and finding startling new information about it. Heck, only a *few years ago*, linguist and lexicographer Ben Zimmer revealed in a column on *Slate* that the word "meh" might be Yiddish, as evidenced in a newly rediscovered Yiddish dictionary from 1928.

Here are other simple but useful Yiddish words and their connotational translations:

- *BASHERT:* kismet or "meant to be," especially in love
- *FAKAKTA:* messed up, not very good
- *GENUG IZ GENUG!:* Enough is enough!
- KLUTZ: clumsy person
- KVETCH: whine
- LUFTMENSCH: person with head in clouds, a dreamer
- MAZEL TOV!: Congrats!
- *NARISHKEIT:* trivial nonsense
- OY VEY! (SOMETIMES *"OY VEY IZ MIR!"* OR *"OY GEVALT!"*): Oh no!
- TUCHUS: buttocks

Considering the Sturm und Drang surrounding what it truly means to be punk, perhaps there's some semblance of an answer to be found among these solidly supersonic superlatives:

- **CARRIE BROWNSTEIN:** Also notable for co-creating the hit television show *Portlandia*, Brownstein was first catapulted into the public eye as a mid-1990s punker whose band Sleater-Kinney acted as a bridge between the radical feminist riot grrrl contingent of the late-1980s Northwest music scene and the more mainstream indie rock that followed.

- **RICHARD HELL:** A pivotal figure in the early punk scene, for both his signature sartorial and tonsorial style, Hell performed with and helped found integral bands of the era, including the Heartbreakers, Television, and the Voidoids.

- **HILLY KRISTAL:** Owned and ran New York City's CBGB from the early 1970s through its closing in 2006; the music venue acted as the social hub and spawning ground for nearly every major (and not-so-major) punk rock group during the raffish scene's prime.

- **"HANDSOME DICK" MANITOBA:** Proto-punk who spearheaded the germinative band the Dictators throughout the mid-1970s and reveled in a form of rocking out that celebrated mid-twentieth-century teenage mayhem like greasy burgers and goofy TV.

- **KEITH MORRIS:** A key force in the hard-core punk scene of the 1980s, Morris formed and fronted such foundational bands as Black Flag and the Circle Jerks, which made punk frenetically faster, ferociously harder, and explosively louder.
- **BUZZ OSBORNE:** A founding member of the Melvins, which innovated a slower, fiercer, and creepier version of punk rock and inspired the "grunge" era to come, particularly Kurt Cobain.
- **JOEY RAMONE:** Cofounded and more or less led what is *the* quintessential American punk group: the Ramones.
- **GENYA RAVAN:** In the 1960s, Ravan fronted the proto-punk Goldie & the Gingerbreads, who were one part Supremes, one part Janis Joplin, one part Carpenters, and all female.
- **LOU REED:** Although not the progenitor of punk rock music, to many aficionados this front man for the immensely influential Velvet Underground was and always will be to the genre what Elvis was to early rock and roll: *the KING*.
- **TINA WEYMOUTH:** Founding member of and bassist for Talking Heads, which portended post-punk's New Wave, largely recasting the genre as more radio-friendly and accessible throughout the 1980s.

Amerikaners

- Cookies commonly known as "black-and-whites," "half-moons," or "harlequins"
- Likely brought to New York at the turn of the twentieth century by German immigrants
- Referred to as "a wonderful thing" in a 1994 episode of *Seinfeld*

Frosted with mathematically equitable vanilla and chocolate fondant atop a round, flat, and subtly lemon-infused sponge cake, "no other cookie is more inextricable from the American Jewish identity," according to *Tablet* as recently as 2015. Now, there are certainly Jewish culinary curiosities that may not be to everyone's taste. But black-and-whites are a tasty treat that even the most persnickety palate may find pleasant.

LEARN MORE: *The Marvelous Mrs. Maisel* featured this soft and sweet morsel in its first episode when protagonist Midge orders two: one for herself and one for the doorman at her building. It wasn't long before *Mrs. Maisel* came to life in a series of pop-up Jewish delicatessens—including one hosted by the famed Carnegie Deli—that, of course, featured the scrumptious black-and-whites.

Analyzing, Analyzing, Analyzing

➤ Also known as "going down the rabbit hole"
➤ Can lead to: pacing, restless slumber, regrettable emails, and highly acclaimed introspective stand-up comedy specials

Four millennia of persecution, forced nomadism, and risk of near total loss of culture have understandably fostered a proclivity for constant analysis. So much so that author and scholar Rabbi Joseph Telushkin refers to Jews as "optimists with worried looks." In fact, the term "Talmudic" was at one time employed by the likes of esteemed twentieth-century journalist H. L. Mencken to mean "bookish" or "studious." And for good reason: Jews have long been considered restless seekers who question, scrutinize, and inquire, but, as Groucho Marx and Larry David would say, "Whatever works!"

LEARN MORE: Exemplars of Jewish overanalyzing on-screen: Missy Foreman-Greenwald's regular bouts of *shpilkes*[5] over the rigors of pubescence on the animated Netflix series *Big Mouth*; David Thewlis's career-making film-length rankled rant about all-life-as-we-know-it in notable Jewish director Mike Leigh's award-winning 1993 film *Naked*; and Dustin Hoffman's ersatz Bob Dylan avatar "Georgie Soloway" in 1971's *Who Is Harry Kellerman and Why Is He Saying Those Terrible Things About Me?*

5 Tornadic state of anxiety

Annie Hall

- Released by United Artists on April 20, 1977
- Winner of 1978 Oscars for Best: Picture, Actress, Director, Original Screenplay
- The transitional picture for director Woody Allen away from his more free-associative early works

Opening with a one-liner recalling two *yentas* kvetching about "the terrible food . . . and such small portions!", *Annie Hall* set the stage for modern-day rom-coms and on-screen Jewish humor alike. Without the rousing critical and commercial success of *Annie Hall*, could there have later been *When Harry Met Sally . . .* or *Seinfeld* or *Curb Your Enthusiasm*? We'll never know. What we *do* know is that *Annie Hall* is likely the funniest movie ever to include multiple references to and clips from the "four-hour documentary on Nazis," *The Sorrow and the Pity*.

LEARN MORE: Frequently invoked in conversations about separating the art from the artist, *Annie Hall* had a significant impact upon release and continued to be the subject of deep dives for decades to come. Such works include: star Diane Keaton's 2011 memoir *Then Again* or Peter Biskind's definitive and marvelously readable history of the 1970s film scene, *Easy Riders, Raging Bulls*. For a somewhat updated *Annie Hall* sans the presence of Woody Allen, there's indie darling shockmeister Todd Solondz's first feature *Fear, Anxiety and Depression*.

Apatow, Judd

- Born December 6, 1967, in Flushing, New York
- Shares a Grammy nom for co-writing "Walk Hard" from *Walk Hard: The Dewey Cox Story*
- Apatow is largely responsible for launching the careers of a vast swath of twenty-first-century funny folks

Right out of the gate, Apatow was a self-avowed comedy diehard, who once wrote an entire term paper about the Marx Brothers . . . just because he felt like it. Apatow began writing for such headliners as Roseanne Barr and Garry Shandling, before signing on as a writer-producer for Shandling's comedy-world-shifting television series *The Larry Sanders Show*. Apatow then co-wrote and produced films that became 1990s mainstays such as *Heavyweights* and *The Cable Guy*, executive produced the TV series *The Ben Stiller Show* and *Freaks & Geeks*, and finally throttled into the early 2000s by directing and writing hit comedy movies such as *Knocked Up*.

LEARN MORE: In addition to his characteristically semi-autobiographical films, the curious can discover plenty more about Apatow in his extensive collection of transcribed one-on-one interviews with fellow funny people, *Sick in the Head: Conversations About Life and Comedy*.

Babka

- Originates from nineteenth-century Jewish communities in Eastern Europe
- Originally made using repurposed leftover dough from challah bread
- First became popular outside Poland and Ukraine in the mid-twentieth century, coincidentally around the time chocolate became the predominant filling

This rich and tasty pastry is made from yeast-leavened dough slathered in sweet filling (typically chocolate, fruit, cinnamon, or cheese) before it's folded over, plaited, baked, then drenched in sugary syrup. It's hard to know for certain exactly where the word "babka" came from, though one theory is that it had something to do with grandmothers. The word "baba" is Slavic for "grandma" and was in fact the original name of the heavenly confection. It was when the humongous pastries were downsized to the more modern parameters that the name changed: hence, "babka" or "little grandmother." The folding of the dough may have also been referencing *Bubbe*'s traditionally pleated skirts. We'll never know for sure, but what *really* matters is: *mmmmm . . . babbbbbka.*

> **LEARN MORE:** Paul Hollywood and fellow televised bakers make an updated version of babka—think more along the lines of a chocolate-swirled coffee cake—on episode 3, season 4 of *The Great British Baking Show.*

Ben & Jerry's

- Ice creamery founded May 5, 1978, in Burlington, Vermont
- The first store was built in a refurbished gas station
- Now in 650 locations in more than thirty-five countries

When Bennett Cohen's plans for medical school fell through, he and childhood friend Jerry Greenfield took a correspondence course to learn how to make their own ice cream. Their trademark became mixing sizable sugary morsels into their recipes. This was due to Cohen's anosmia, which leaves him without a sense of smell and in want of diverse *tactile* stimulation. Although they no longer have operational control of the scrappily ragtag ice cream company (it was scooped up by Unilever in 2000), Cohen and Greenfield remain vocal supporters of their sweet brainchild as well as its socially and environmentally conscious ethos. As recently as July 2021, Cohen and Greenfield wrote in an *New York Times* op-ed, "We are the founders of Ben & Jerry's. We are also proud Jews. It's part of who we are and how we've identified ourselves for our whole lives."

> **LEARN MORE:** To sample further tasty Ben & Jerry's history, read 1995's *Ben & Jerry's: The Inside Scoop*, authored by erstwhile CEO Fred "Chico" Lager, or Cohen and Greenfield's own *Ben & Jerry's Double-Dip*, published in 1998.

Bernhardt, Sarah

- Born Henriette-Rosine Bernard, October 1844, in Paris, France
- Known in her time as "*la Divine Sarah*"
- Considered the first globally renowned theater star

The illegitimate daughter of a Jewish Dutch courtesan, Sarah Bernhardt was brought up in a convent with the intention of becoming a nun until—at age sixteen—she was encouraged by a close relative of Napoleon to pursue acting at the Paris Conservatoire. A young firebrand, she would exit two years later after finding the institution's methodologies to be outdated. Her characteristically flippant response to anti-Semitic criticism of her "Jewish" accent was thus:

"I am a daughter of the great Jewish race, and my somewhat uncultivated language is the outcome of our enforced wanderings." And wander Bernhardt did, everywhere she could find a stage on which to perform all manner of roles. She was not only an actress but playwright, essayist, and costume/set designer. Among her most dedicated fans were the likes of Alexandre Dumas, Victor Hugo, and Mark Twain. It was Twain who opined that there are five kinds of actresses, "bad actresses, fair actresses, good actresses, great actresses—and then there's Sarah Bernhardt."

LEARN MORE: For more Sarah divinity, there's 1907's *My Double Life: The Memoirs of Sarah Bernhardt.*

Bialy

- A chewy, imperfectly round yeast roll rather like a bagel . . . but much flatter
- Name is a diminutive of *bialystoker kuchen*, paying homage to its Polish town of origin, Bialystok, buttressed by the Yiddish word for "baked good," specifically "cake"
- Jewish Polish immigrants first brought the bialy to the United States in the late nineteenth century

Unlike a bagel, a bialy is not boiled before it's baked, and, in lieu of a hole, its center indentation is filled with diced onions and savory spices. Be that as it may, many believe there is only room for *one* roundish baked breadstuff at the breakfast table these days. And while the bagel may have won the popular vote, "the bialy is more of a secret love," as Jane Ziegelman, the director of the Tenement Museum's culinary program, put it in 2018. There's even been an entire *book* written by *New York Times* restaurant critic Mimi Sheraton chronicling the rise and fall of the bialy, *The Bialy Eaters*.

LEARN MORE: New York City's Kossar's Bagels & Bialys remains the oldest bialy bakery in the United States, having opened in 1936 originally as Kossar's Bialystoker Kuchen Bakery. It's still right there at 367 Grand Street for those who want to sample the real McCoy when it comes to the rare but taste bud–titillating bialy.

Blanc, Mel

- Born Melvin Jerome Blank on May 30, 1908, in San Francisco, California
- A radio broadcast prodigy at nineteen, he became the most impactful voice actor in animation history
- Featured as nearly every character throughout the foundational *Looney Tunes/Merrie Melodies* cartoon universe, including Bugs Bunny, Daffy Duck, and Porky Pig

That's *not* all, folks. Blanc took the entertainment world by storm when he was prominently featured on such formative series as *The Jack Benny Show, The George Burns and Gracie Allen Show*, and *The Abbott and Costello Show*. This early work was the opening red curtain on a career that lasted a jam-packed seven decades. Far more a Yosemite Sam than Tweety Bird[6] when it came to navigating early Hollywood's notorious business side, Blanc was the first voice actor to receive on-screen credit. Blanc later learned through a medical examination that his vocal cords were uniquely powerful, hence his uncanny abilities. Evidently, he passed this talent along to his son, Noel, who successfully took up the torch upon his father's passing in 1989.[7]

> **LEARN MORE:** Read all about Blanc's raucous adventures voicing virtually all of the twentieth century's most well-known cartoon characters in publisher and pop culture historian Ben Ohmart's 2012 biography *Mel Blanc: The Man of a Thousand Voices*.

6 Both of whom he voiced
7 Voicing the likes of Elmer Fudd, the Tasmanian Devil, and Porky Pig

Blintzes

- Name stems from the Slavic-Yiddish word "*blintse*" or "pancake"
- Ritualistically served on the holiday of Shavuot ("Feast of Weeks"), celebrating the Jewish people receiving the Torah through Moses at Mount Sinai *or* whenever else someone really wants a blintz

Essentially crepes that have been filled with a serenely sweetened,[8] creamily spreadable cheese[9] before being pan-fried to a sun-kissed golden brown, blintzes are more than a delicious treat. The natural nostalgia of the pastry also makes them a fine conversation starter, as was the case during a 2007 *Esquire* feature interview. Self-identifying Jewish Clevelander and journalist Scott Raab conversed with award-winning actor Paul Giamatti[10] . . . and spent virtually the entire discussion talking about and eating blintzes. Then there's the *New York Times* revealing in December 2021 that Arlo Guthrie, Jewish son of traveling troubadour Woody Guthrie, had been wooed by his current wife when she first made his grandma's recipe for blintzes. How sweet is that?

LEARN MORE: Get artful with Carol D. Brent's 1976 *Crepes: The Fine Art of Crepe and Blintz Cooking.* Or, get the full story of blintzes and Shavuot as accessibly as possible in Barbara Diamond Goldin's 2012 children's book *A Mountain of Blintzes.*

---

8   By combining it with egg, sugar, and vanilla
9   Usually: cream cheese, farmer cheese, cottage cheese, ricotta, mascarpone, or even crème fraîche
10 Not Jewish . . . but his wife and son are!

Borscht

- A somewhat sour, somewhat tangy, somewhat savory claret-colored soup made predominantly from ruby red beetroots
- Served either hot or cold, vegetarian or *fleischig*[11]-based
- Makes for a refreshingly hearty health drink

Typically prepared through a traditional Russian methodology: a kind of "slow cooking"—be it boiling, broiling, or sautéing the beets and their companion vegetables to make a unified stock. To this you can add all manner of potential garnish: potatoes, egg yolks, chives, parsley, scallions, and, of course, the pièce de résistance, *smetana*.[12] Borscht goes back to ancient times when it was first made with stems, leaves, and cow parsnip (basically grass), before its "modern" beet-based iteration burbled up in Ukraine. Initially brought over to the United States in the late nineteenth century by Russian Jews escaping religious persecution, along with their fellow borscht-lovers, the Mennonites.

> LEARN MORE: Leda Schubert and Bonnie Christensen's 2011 children's book *The Princess of Borscht* may not have much to say about the lengthy history of the nearly infinite recipes for borscht, but with a title and cover that are utterly adorable, how can you pass it up?

---

11 Meat; though literally translates to "flesh"
12 Like sour cream . . . but much, much thinner and runnier

Borscht Belt

- Also known as "the Jewish Alps"
- Encompassed as many as five hundred resorts in the Catskill Mountains of New York
- Took its name from the Eastern European beet soup that was a popular staple of the resorts

Jews from New York City flocked to this network of bungalows, summer camps, and cabins in the late nineteenth century, due in large part to the fact that they were not welcomed at many of the hotels in the city. These days, the Borscht Belt is no more. Its swarm of Jewish sanctuaries for fun, frolic, and foodie-ness began fading out in the late 1960s, before going almost entirely defunct by the 1990s. But in its heyday, it was the ultimate Cuisinart of the best of Jewish culture: from culinary, to entertainment (especially live comedy), to cabaret and singing. The Borscht Belt reared comedians including Morey Amsterdam, Shelley Berman, Rodney Dangerfield, Totie Fields, Estelle Getty, Shecky Greene, Robert Klein, Jackie Mason, Jonathan Winters, and the incomparable Henny Youngman.

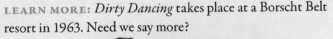

LEARN MORE: *Dirty Dancing* takes place at a Borscht Belt resort in 1963. Need we say more?

Brisket

- A prime cut of beef from the lower section of the cow's chest
- The word dates back to fourteenth-century Middle English's "*brusket*," itself likely evolved from "*bjorsk*"— Old Norse for "cartilage"
- Can be prepared as pastrami, corned beef, pot roast, and pho

When *Sex and the City*'s Harry Goldenblatt saw his loving girlfriend had made brisket for their first Shabbat together, it meant a wedding was in their future. Eighteenth-century Central and Eastern Europeans were the first to put a Jewish stamp on brisket, slow cooking and braising the beef before serving it hot for holidays such as Rosh Hashanah, Passover, Chanukah, and—as with Harry and Charlotte—Shabbat. For twentieth-century Jewish Americans especially, brisket became "the most important meat, period," according to Brooklyn-based Mile End Deli's Noah Bernamoff, during a 2014 Center for Jewish History panel discussion. "Name any Jewish holiday," Bernamoff continued, "and they'll tell you they ate brisket during that holiday."

LEARN MORE: For even more helpings of brisket, you can slice your way through James Beard Award winner and rabbi Gil Marks's comprehensive *Encyclopedia of Jewish Food*, published in 2010. Or if you're in New York City at the right time, there's the annual "Brisket King" competition to attend.

Brooks, Mel

- Born Melvin Kaminsky on June 28, 1926, in Brooklyn, New York
- Known for genre-shattering laugh riots including *Blazing Saddles*, *Young Frankenstein*, and *The Producers*
- An uber-rare EGOT (Emmy/Grammy/Oscar/Tony Award) winner

Comedy legend Mel Brooks was inspired by the Marx Brothers, his early mentor Sid Caesar, and longtime collaborators Carl Reiner, Buck Henry, Gene Wilder, Marty Feldman, and Madeline Kahn. He's the definitive link in the century-long evolution from classic Jewish comedians of the vaudeville/Borscht Belt era to today's congregation of multihyphenates such as Billy Crystal, Jenny Slate, Jon Stewart, Nick Kroll, and Tracee Ellis Ross. Brooks has successfully tackled a little bit of *everything*, from stand-up comedy to co-creating the TV series *Get Smart*, to producing David Lynch's *The Elephant Man* and Jeff Goldblum starrer *The Fly*. His films were consistently regarded as bellwethers for where comedy movies would be heading next.

LEARN MORE: In addition to reading 2021's extensive autobiography *All About Me!* and watching the 2019 documentary *Mel Brooks: Make a Noise*, the inquisitive can peek into some next-gen Brooks through the works of Mel's son Max—creator of *The Zombie Survival Guide* and *World War Z*.

Bruce, Lenny

- Born Leonard Alfred Schneider on October 13, 1925, in New York
- The original subversive king of stand-up comedy known for eschewing contemporary societal inhibitions for onstage material
- Introduced as "the most shocking comedian of our time" by Steve Allen on late-night television in 1959

Lenny Bruce courted an equal parts heroic and reckless brinkmanship in his career (and life) until his untimely passing via morphine overdose in late 1966. Bruce worked into his ever-changing act bebop-influenced cadences, acerbic political and religious commentary, provocatively prurient perspectives, and as many Yiddish words as profane ones. But it was the profane language that led to multiple arrests for obscenity, blacklisting from the public forum, a devastating downfall, and ultimately posthumous reevaluation and elevation to martyred comedy hero. In 2003, Bruce was officially pardoned for his obscenity charges by New York Governor George Pataki. A year later, Comedy Central voted him the third greatest stand-up comedian of all time after George Carlin and Richard Pryor . . . both of whom cited Bruce as a major influence.

LEARN MORE: Strap in for Bruce's 1967 autobiography *How to Talk Dirty and Influence People*, and Bob Fosse's impressionistic 1974 Academy Award–nominated film *Lenny*.

Burns, George

- Cigar-wielding seminal entertainer né Nathan Birnbaum
- Born January 20, 1896, in New York City
- His lengthy show business tenure spanned the evolution of vaudeville, radio, television, and cinema

As George Burns frames it in the opening pages of his 1976 memoir *Living It Up*, "Getting to be my age didn't happen overnight." His unconventionally active career lasted until his passing at the age of one hundred. Burns enjoyed monumental success in just about every existing art form, including covering the likes of the Beatles and the Rolling Stones as a singer. He broke all manner of records when it came to radio broadcast listenership, defined exactly what a television sitcom could be, penned bestselling memoir after bestselling memoir, thrice portrayed the Almighty "big G" on-screen, and earned an Oscar for Best Supporting Actor for his role in 1975's *The Sunshine Boys*. Burns proved the truth in his own sage pronouncement in those selfsame opening pages from his memoir: "Getting old doesn't mean that you have to stop having fun."

LEARN MORE: You'll quite literally get the most out of George Burns in the 1991 autobiography omnibus *The Most of George Burns*.

Camp Firewood

- Setting for the 2001 cult classic film *Wet Hot American Summer*
- Based on Jewish co-creators David Wain's and Michael Showalter's own childhood memories
- Wain notably attended Camp Modin, the oldest Jewish summer camp still in existence[13]

It's never *explicitly* stated that Firewood is a *Jewish* summer camp. But just *try* to convince the film's legion of fans otherwise. Hard evidence? Camp director Beth's conspicuous roll call: "Amanda Klein, Jessica Azaria, Ira Stevenberg..." How about camp radio show host Arty "The Beekeeper" Solomon's Henny Youngman[14]–style one-liners, including the one about "Rabbi Rothstein"? The big talent show is meanwhile emceed by fellow Youngman-esque entertainer Alan Shemper, whose groan-inducing corniness is straight out of the 1980s bar mitzvah performers' playbook. No wonder *Tablet* designated *Wet Hot* "the defining Jewish summer camp movie."

> **LEARN MORE:** Hit the ol' brambly trail for further wet and Wainy adventures at Camp Firewood in the two Netflix companion series *First Day of Camp* and *Ten Years Later*, or the documentary *Hurricane of Fun: The Making of Wet Hot*.

---

13 After a century in operation, as of 2022
14 Foundational vaudeville/Borscht Belt performer known for his rapid-fire "Take my wife, please..." brand of joke-telling

Chabad Centers

- Established in 1775 by Rabbi Schneur Zalman
- Originally grew and flourished out of the town Lubavitch
- As of 2020, 3,500 Chabad centers can be found in more than one hundred countries around the world

The name Chabad is a concision of the Hebrew words for the movement's core mission values: *Chochmah*, *Binah*, *Da'at*, meaning "Wisdom, Understanding, and Knowledge." This movement primarily grew out of the efforts of late eighteenth-century Hasidic[15] Jewish community members to preserve Torah-based practices while under a restrictive, oppressive regime. Today it is one of the largest of such community outreach organizations. Genre-bending reggae-rocker Matisyahu was deeply embedded in the globe-stretching Chabad community throughout his chart-breaking music career. The support that nomadic Matisyahu received from Chabad facilities as a launchpad for his breakthrough into the mainstream music scene is just one example of the empowerment such centers can offer.

> **LEARN MORE:** Rabbi and *New York Times* bestselling author Chaim Potok laid bare his reflections on growing up a part of the Lubavitch community in the Crown Heights neighborhood of Brooklyn, in 1972's National Book Award–nominated *My Name Is Asher Lev*.

---

15 Literally "pious ones," the Hasidic movement teaches strict adherence to Talmudic law and grew out of eighteenth-century Eastern Europe before spreading across the globe

Challah

- Pronounced "hah-luh" and meaning "portion" in Hebrew
- A subtly sweet, hoagie-sized loaf of *lechem*[16] with a glistening amber-brass hue
- Often braided with twelve humps symbolizing the twelve tribes of Israel

Contemporary observant Jews will ritually set aflame a bit of dough in the oven before baking their challah, which is served on holy days like Shabbat, as well as during weddings or bar and bat mitzvahs. This long-held tradition traces back to the Torah, which dictates that a portion of dough be set aside as tribute to local *cohanim*.[17] Dairy-free and made with egg yolks, the texture and taste is similar to a spongy French brioche with a muted hint of tanginess, thanks to an inconspicuous dollop of honey in its batter. Challah can also be studded with raisins, poppy seeds, or sesame seeds, and include sugar instead of honey. However, one must be *very* careful not to overdo the sweetness lest one end up with cake instead of bread. This would require a whole other blessing, a *mezonot*, instead of the hamotzi.

> **LEARN MORE:** "Challah" back[18] at Rochie Pinson and her 2017 book *Rising: The Book of Challah*.

16 Bread
17 Jewish priests
18 You *knew* it was coming

Chocolate Gelt

- Also known as *dmei Chanukah* and *Hanukkah gelt*
- Faux-gold- or faux-silver-wrapped chocolate coins given out during the festival of Chanukah
- May be awarded as the prize for winning the traditional top-spinning game of dreidel

In the 1700s, actual money was given to children, who were expected to pass along the gift to their teachers as a form of Chanukah gift. Later, this was replaced by a new tradition involving various-sized chocolate coins packed up tightly in small mesh pouches that resemble money bags flounced around haplessly in swashbuckling adventure flicks. In the 1920s, candy manufacturers realized they could make a killing mass-producing these simple chocolate coins. Profits boomed so high that the first American manufacturer, Loft's, was able to purchase Pepsi a mere ten years later and form what we know of today as PepsiCo.

LEARN MORE: Indulge in the surprisingly circuitous journey of chocolate gelt, courtesy of Rabbi Deborah Prinz's 2012 book *On the Chocolate Trail: A Delicious Adventure Connecting Jews, Religions, History, Travel, Rituals and Recipes to the Magic of Cacao*. Or, if you're in the neighborhood, find a seat at one of Rabbi Prinz's many speaking engagements in which she takes on the enviable role of globetrotting lecturer on the tasty intersection of chocolate and religion.

Chopped Liver

- A take on liver pâté originating in medieval Germany
- A staple of many Jewish deli menus
- Served as a sandwich, as a dip for cucumbers, or as a spread on matzo

The main ingredients ground together include onions, salt, pepper, hard-boiled eggs, schmaltz, and, of course, liver, usually from beef or chicken. Chopped liver has suffered quite the bad rap over the years. *"What am I? CHOPPED LIVER?!"* The *liver* in chopped liver is actually one of the most nutrient-dense sources of protein on the planet. It's also extremely high in vitamins A and B, iron, folate, and . . . copper. That said, caveat emptor when it comes to the *chopped* variety of the stuff. Eating an excess amount can exacerbate gout, arthritis, and heart complications due to the generous inclusion of schmaltz. To paraphrase the beer companies: "Gorge responsibly."

LEARN MORE: For those members of the eco-friendly set who still crave the uniquely tasting and silky-smooth texture of chopped liver, there do exist vegetarian and vegan alternatives to the long-held recipe. Such seemingly quirky concepts are catalogued in the "Jewish Food Hero" book collection, such as *Beyond Chopped Liver: 59 Jewish Recipes Get a Vegan Health Makeover*.

Davis, Sammy Jr.

- Born December 8, 1925, in Harlem
- Grammy and Emmy Award–winning singer, dancer, actor, comedian, and film/television producer
- Member of the rip-roaringly rambunctious Las Vegas entertainers known as the Rat Pack

It was at the ripe age of three that Davis began the widely hailed, widely beloved, and widely diverse show business career that would eventually land him both a Kennedy Center Honor and, posthumously, the Grammy Lifetime Achievement Award. By 1960, he was starring in the original *Ocean's 11* alongside fellow Rat Pack members Frank Sinatra, Dean Martin, Peter Lawford, and Joey Bishop. Davis began his *other* lifelong journey as a mensch[19] of great Jewish faith and pride while in the hospital recovering from the loss of his eye at the age of twenty-nine. Davis found solace after reading about the Jewish people's four-thousand-year struggle and innate resilience as captured in Abram L. Sachar's *A History of the Jews*.

LEARN MORE: Davis (co-)wrote *four* autobiographies, most notably 1965's *Yes, I Can*. PBS also aired the documentary *Sammy Davis, Jr: I've Gotta Be Me* in 2017.

19 A person of great integrity

Delighting in Delis

When it comes to Jewish gastronomic contributions, there's renowned chef Mike Solomonov, celebrity manager Shep Gordon who was an impetus for the launch of the Food Network, *and* this wide-spanning variety of delis where you can eat all the goodies you'd ever hope for:

- **CANTER'S DELI:** opened in Los Angeles in 1931, it's known as much for its menu[20] as for the famous clientele who might be sitting at the booth next to yours
- **CARNEGIE DELI:** opened in 1937 right offstage the world-famous Midwest Manhattan theater district and became a major celebrity hotspot during its heyday
- **IZZY'S:** the first kosher-style delicatessen west of the Allegheny Mountains in 1901, it's consistently voted a local best in Cincinnati more than a century later
- **KATZ'S DELICATESSEN**[21]**:** this Manhattan Lower East Side eatery has been known for its towering "mile-high" corned beef and pastrami sandwiches since opening in 1888
- **LANGER'S DELI:** this Los Angeles purveyor of traditional Jewish comfort food claimed in a 2018 *Los Angeles Times* feature that they've served more than ten million pounds of pastrami

---

20 The *Financial Times* referred to Canter's as one of the fifty best "food stores" in the world in 2021

21 *This* is the restaurant where Meg Ryan's "Sally" loudly acts out for Billy Crystal's "Harry" how women are able to fake physical enjoyment so authentically in the bedroom; there is indeed a sign outside that reads: *"Where Harry met Sally . . . Hope you have what she had!"*

- **NATE 'N AL'S:** Beverly Hills–based eatery that opened in 1945 and was long a socializing hub for some of Hollywood's biggest and brightest stars in need of a hearty bowl of matzo ball soup or a Reuben sandwich
- **RUSS & DAUGHTERS:** New York City's iconic Lower East Side–based provider of fresh fish, baked pastries, and specialty foods that has been run by the same family for four generations
- **SHAPIRO'S DELICATESSEN:** regularly listed among the top ten delis nationwide by the likes of *USA Today* and *The Nosher*, this family-run Indianapolis-based eatery has been a staple of the culinary scene since 1905

Denver's West Side

- As of 2020, one-third of all Jews in Colorado live in the Denver area
- This is a total of nearly fifteen thousand households
- For this reason, its Colfax Viaduct received the nickname "the Jewish Passover"

As the oldest Jewish enclave in Denver, the West Side thrived with Jewish life in the mid-twentieth century. It was home to bustling kosher marketplaces, its own eruv[22] still recognized by city ordinance, and a teenage girl named Golda Meir who would grow up to become Israel's first (and only, to date) female prime minister. According to the University of Denver's Dr. Jeanne Abrams, although numbers of Jews in the area have dwindled over the past few decades, communal goodwill and observance of tradition still bond what remains a tight-knit Jewish community. There remains a robust congregation of Orthodox Jews who have established a yeshiva high school, Jewish girls' high school, and graduate school for advanced Jewish study.

LEARN MORE: You can read up on Denver's Jewish "West Side Stories" in prolific historian Phil Goodstein's 2011 book *North Side Story*, or watch and listen to them in documentarian Steven Feld's slightly more appropriately titled *West Side Stories*, also released in 2011.

22 Find out more on page 35

Doja Cat

- Born October 21, 1995, in Los Angeles
- Grammy Award–winning singer, performer, producer, and viral Internet sensation
- Her song with Nicki Minaj, "Say So," was the first by a female rap duo to hit #1 on the US singles chart

Amala Ratna Zandile Dlamini chose the stage name Doja Cat to denote her fealty to both cats and doja—rapper argot for, well, *weed*. For her birth name, her South African father and Jewish American mother anointed her with the grafting of "Amala" and "Ratna," Sanskrit for "pure" and "gem," respectively. "Ratna" also describes someone who is original, resourceful, and mindful of everything in life being interconnected. Not a bad depiction of a self-made Internet star who has gone on to "be fruitful and multiply" across the entertainment scene as per the Hebrew blessing . . . and translation of her Zulu middle name, "Zandile."

> **LEARN MORE:** Doja Cat has pronounced 2021's *Planet Her* the first album that fully embraces her true identity as an artist. Considering it's named after an imaginary planet she conjured as part of her stage/online persona, *Planet Her* is as good a place as any from which to launch your journey into Doja Cat's universe.

Dr. Katz, Professional Therapist

- Created and voiced by Jewish stand-up comic/folk singer Jonathan Katz
- First appearance: 1994's one-minute short segments on *Short Attention Span Theater*
- Dr. Katz made it to a full series on May 28, 1995

Jonathan Katz hit pay dirt with this cartoon about the quotidian goings-on of a harried therapist. Though it pays respectful homage to 1970s precursor *The Bob Newhart Show*, unlike that series' protagonist, Manhattan-based Dr. Katz spends *his* therapy sessions acting more as showcase impresario than straight man to actual stand-up comedians quite literally voicing their bits. Dr. Katz must meanwhile put up with his sardonic receptionist, voiced by Laura Silverman (Sarah Silverman's sister). And he struggles through his relationship with his live-in twentysomething son, Benjamin. Voiced by H. Jon Benjamin, Benny is quick-witted but also rather lost on his path toward adulthood. He's in ironic need of, well, a good therapist.

LEARN MORE: The real-life Katz has traveled around the country speaking about and performing his show onstage. One exhibition was 2007's taped *An Evening with Dr. Katz: Live from the Comedy Central Stage*. Audible continued the series via audio-only segments in 2017.

Dylan, Bob

- Born Robert Allen Zimmerman on May 24, 1941, in Duluth, Minnesota
- In 1999, one of *Time* magazine's "100 Most Important People" of the twenty-first century
- Received 2016's Nobel Prize for Literature for his song lyrics

Nobel Prize committee member Professor Horace Engdahl referred to Dylan as "a singer worthy of a place beside ... the Romantic visionaries, beside the kings and queens of the Blues, beside the forgotten masters of brilliant standards." Dylan became for millions around the planet a vital new *kulturbärare*[23] ... even if he wasn't exactly thrilled about the role. Just as Dylan ruffled some feathers when he transitioned from folk to electric guitar in 1965, he surprised the world with his Christian conversion in the late 1970s, even releasing a series of gospel records ... before re-embracing his Jewish heritage in the early 1980s.

LEARN MORE: Although the troubadour's been notoriously reclusive, there are plenty of Dylan resources available—most prominently: DA Pennebaker's pioneering 1967 cinema vérité documentary *Don't Look Back*, Todd Haynes's 2007 experimental biopic *I'm Not There*, and Dylan's own private literary musings via his *Chronicles* series.

23 "Culture bearer"—someone who moves the culture as a whole forward

Egg Cream

❧ Like an ice cream soda—sans the ice cream

❧ Popularized by New York Jewish immigrant Louis Auster in the 1920s

❧ Don't be fooled: an egg cream is made with neither egg nor cream

Made of seltzer, milk, and chocolate or vanilla syrup, egg cream may be a corruption of the Yiddish "echt," which roughly translates to "genuine" or "real," as in the egg cream being the "*real* McCoy" or "*genuine* article." There also *was* a possible creamy drink forebearer served in the 1880s that included egg as a thickening agent before refrigerating milk was more common. Culture historian Andrew Coe has speculated that the quick-fix thirst quencher allowed poorer Jewish immigrants in Brooklyn and the Lower East Side to feel as though they could drink something comparable to the fancier homemade sodas being served Uptown . . . but for a Downtown cost.

LEARN MORE: There's Barry Joseph's book *Seltzertopia*, Coe's own documentary *Egg Cream*, and Elliot Willensky's *When Brooklyn Was the World (1920–1957)*, which includes a line suggesting that back in the day, to have a candy store or soda shop without an egg cream on the list of offerings would be unthinkable (at least in Brooklyn).

Eruv

- Hebrew word that roughly translates to "overlapping"
- Refers to a territory partitioned by a bordering wire that symbolically expands one's home perimeter into the public space
- The exact specifications for eruvim have been a source of controversy throughout the two thousand years they've existed

Even when it comes to the very act of *being Jewish*, Jews can find a way to navigate their own path. Which is where the handily utilitarian eruv comes into play. By extending the home, an eruv wire helps many sidestep the religious law that forbids carrying anything from a private to a public zone, or anything at all over six feet in length in a public space, during Sabbath, the day of rest. If you're an observant Jew—particularly an Orthodox one—and you need to carry your wallet, car keys, or *baby* with you from the house to shul on the Sabbath, thanks to an eruv being set up around your village, now you can.

LEARN MORE: Most of Manhattan is surrounded by a clear wire, the *most expensive* of the two hundred city-sized eruvim worldwide. At $125,000 to $150,000 per annum to keep the wire maintained, New York City's eruv is obviously worth a gander.

Fairfax District, Los Angeles

- Also known as "Beverly-Fairfax"[24]
- A 3.2-square-mile Central Los Angeles neighborhood
- Jewish virtuoso record producer Phil Spector started his first rock group—the Teddy Bears—while enrolled at Fairfax High School

In the 1920s and 1930s, Jews who had originally congregated in high numbers in nearby Boyle Heights moved in droves to Fairfax. They established four synagogues by 1935, tripling that number within a decade. It is home to the Holocaust Museum LA.[25] The area also hosts such secular commercial cultural institutions as CBS's broadcasting center and the area's farmers' market. As of October 2018, after a two-year grassroots activist campaign, the area is preserved on the National Register of Historic Places.

> **LEARN MORE:** Like the Jews who ultimately joined its exodus, the world-famous Canter's Deli moved from Boyle Heights to the Fairfax District where it acts not only as a delicious delicatessen but also as a living tribute to the history of the area's Jewish community.

---

24 So called due to its center being at the intersection of Beverly Blvd. and Fairfax Ave.
25 The oldest museum of its kind in the US, founded in 1961

Fiddler on the Roof

- 1964 stage musical and winner of nine Tonys
- Music by Jerry Bock, lyrics by Sheldon Harnick, and book by Joseph Stein
- Adapted into a just-as-monumentally-successful film in 1971

The musical is based on Arnold Perl's play *Tevye and His Daughters*, itself an adaptation of Yiddish author/playwright Sholem Aleichem's[26] turn-of-the-twentieth-century shtetl stories of Ukrainian Jewish everyman Tevye the Dairyman.[27] Centered on the notion that one may live in struggle yet remain boisterously hopeful, you'd be hard-pressed to find a modern-day work of creative expression as closely associated with Jewish culture. Disparate communities worldwide—Jewish or not—have found such great wisdom and lyricism in the play that many believe (at least until COVID-19) *Fiddler* played *somewhere* on the planet *every day* since first opening on Broadway.

LEARN MORE: "Everybody thinks it's about *them*," suggests Broadway legend Joel Grey in the 2019 documentary *Fiddler: A Miracle of Miracles*.

---

26 The nom de plume for Solomon Naumovich Rabinovich
27 Full name Tevye ben Shneur Zalman

Figuring It All Out

Why ask "why"? Some notable Jews made this question the North Star by which they navigated the ship of their lives:

- **HANNAH ARENDT:** author, journalist, Holocaust survivor, and coiner of the phrase "banality of evil"[28] who spent the majority of her life educating herself and others about the behind-the-scenes mechanisms and motivations for totalitarianism, authoritarianism, dictatorships, oppression, and the historical patterns of revolutionary actions

- **WALTER BENJAMIN:** his idiomatic research process via exhaustive notes on philosophy, sociopolitics, and culture were organized over the span of nearly fifteen years into his incomplete but massive *Arcades Project*

- **NOAM CHOMSKY:** prolific, enduring, and influential media analyst, theorist, and linguist who explores the disparity between what we see in various forms of mass media versus what is present in the world around us

- **RAM DASS:** born Richard Alpert; together with his colleague Dr. Timothy Leary, combined Eastern religious concepts with the counterculture 1960s ethos, as illustrated in his book, *Be Here Now*, which inspired Apple's Steve Jobs and Beat poet paterfamilias Lawrence Ferlinghetti

---

28 Arendt's highly controversial notion that suggests that massively evil acts such as genocide are committed not by inhuman monsters, but by average persons who fall sway to a bureaucratic, officious mindset brought on by larger societal pressures (aka "the Nuremberg defense" of "Just doin' our job")

- **JACQUES DERRIDA:** Algerian-French postmodern post-structuralist who popularized the radically disruptive notion of "deconstructionism," which posits that truth and meaning can be seen as subjective, debatable, or perhaps even nonexistent

- **EDMUND HUSSERL:** influential early twentieth-century philosopher who developed an entire field of research known as "phenomenology," to establish a systematic understanding of the unmeasurable and undefinable, like consciousness

- **GYÖRGY LUKÁCS:** a central founder of Western Marxism, focusing much of his research and work on the concept of "class consciousness"

- **KARL MARX:** instead of becoming a rabbi like his paternal forebearers, he became a mid-nineteenth-century popularizer of the economical-political tract of modern-day communism, Marxism

- **SIMONE WEIL:** French philosopher and political activist who joined in on factory lines to better understand and aid the working class

- **LUDWIG WITTGENSTEIN:** his work is considered something of a Rosetta Stone when it comes to the philosophical precepts behind semantics, syntax, grammar, semiotics, rhetorical logic, and our use of words themselves

Finding the Secrets
of the Universe

Here's one humble constellation of Jews, out of many, who have become illuminative stars in the ever-expanding galaxy of science and mathematics:

▚ **MAYIM BIALIK:** not merely someone who has *acted* as a scientist on the hit sitcom *The Big Bang Theory*, Bialik is indeed a full-fledged neuroscientist who promotes programs through which young women can get more involved in STEAM subjects

▚ **ALBERT EINSTEIN:** so renowned is his genius, his surname is a synonym for the word; and he was *funny*, too

▚ **PAUL ERDŐS:** a prolific mathematician who collaborated with an astonishing number of work partners; there remains today a community of such practitioners who identify themselves by their "Erdős Number," denoting how many steps away they are from a co-author of one of Erdős's virtually innumerable co-published papers

▚ **RICHARD FEYNMAN:** Nobel Prize–winning physicist known for his gregarious personality and for mainstreaming science during the 1960s and '70s

- **HEDY LAMARR:** though best known in her lifetime as one of the screen queens of twentieth-century cinema, Lamarr was posthumously championed for also possessing a remarkable talent for and drive toward generating inventive developments in the field of communication technology, especially in the realm of sonar and radar

- **EMMY NOETHER:** German mathematician of the late nineteenth and early twentieth centuries who developed profound leaps in theoretical physics and abstract algebra, for which she was in 1935 dubbed "the most significant creative mathematical genius thus far produced since the higher education of women began" by Einstein

- **CHANDA PRESCOD-WEINSTEIN:** Award-winning author of 2021's *The Disordered Cosmos: A Journey into Dark Matter, Spacetime, and Dreams Deferred* who was recognized by *Essence* magazine in 2019 as one of "15 Black Women Who Are Paving the Way in STEM and Breaking Barriers" and later by *Nature* as one of "ten people who helped shape science in 2020"

- **MARK ZUCKERBERG:** leveraged his prodigious computer, science, and math skills to create an irreconcilable paradigm shift in how humans interact with one another, namely by cofounding Facebook

The Forward

- First issue was published on April 22, 1897
- Originated in New York City
- Named in homage to the German Social Democratic Party publication *Vorwärts* (as in *"Forward, march!"*)

Though no longer a socialist daily for the Yiddish community, *The Forward* holds tight to its roots as a Jewish-focused news source that leans unabashedly to the left. Both its English and Yiddish versions have broadened their scope over the years to include celebrity interviews, regular columns on culturally topical issues, humor pieces, and just about anything else worth knowing about in the Jewish community writ large. It has published online-only since January 17, 2019. *The Forward* remains an outlet Jews—especially American Jews—turn to as, in the words of former editor in chief Jane Eisner, a resource that "tells the American Jewish story better than anyone else."

> **LEARN MORE:** Check in on award-winning filmmaker Marlene Booth's hour-long 1988 documentary *The Forward: From Immigrants to Americans*, which chronicles the entire story of the outlet, including its early *"Bintel* Brief"[29] feature, considered the first precursor of "Dear Abby" columns.[30]

---

29 "Bundle of Letters"
30 Originated not by anyone named Abby, but by Pauline Phillips—*also* a Jew!

Freud, Sigmund

- Born May 6, 1856
- From Příbor, Czechia (today's Czech Republic)
- Neurologist who employed dialogue between patient and doctor—what would soon be called "the talking cure"—to address certain psychological conditions

Though secular, Sigmund Freud notes in his 1927 book *An Autobiographical Study* that Judaism's open-minded tolerance and constant seeking of answers influenced his work, especially in the area of "free association." Aside from the development of modern-day psychology itself, his most enduring legacy can likely be found in his 1930 book *Civilization and Its Discontents*. Freud here tracks the wide-spanning emotional discomfort that arises from the disparity between how people see themselves and how they are perceived by everyone else. The aggravation of that internal conflict by an ever-expanding surrounding society is essentially what Freud meant when discussing a favorite subject: *neuroticism*. Now just imagine what he would have had to say about today's social media.

LEARN MORE: In addition to poring over his 1927 autobiography, curious investigators of Freud can take a gander at David Cronenberg's 2011 biopic *A Dangerous Method* or have a bit of fun with more lighthearted fare chronicling Freud's rowdy misadventures with two heavy metal–obsessed time travelers from the 1980s in *Bill & Ted's Excellent Adventure*.

Friedan, Betty

- Born February 4, 1921, in Peoria, Illinois
- Originally named Bettye Naomi Goldstein
- Cofounder and the first president of the National Organization for Women

Betty Friedan's bestselling 1963 book *The Feminine Mystique* is credited with heralding mainstream awareness of the plight of women, which previously went unrecognized as—in Friedan's summation—"the problem that has no name." After marrying Carl Friedan in 1947, Betty reared three children and embraced the responsibilities of an archetypal housewife while remaining dedicated to her work as a changemaker. "The truth is, I've always been a bad-tempered b----," as she put it in her 2000 memoir *Life So Far*. Fellow feminist icon Germaine Greer concurred in a 2006 elegy of Friedan in *The Guardian*, making sure to add that Betty "changed the course of human history almost single-handedly."

LEARN MORE: The papers of the preternaturally productive Betty Friedan are held at Harvard University's Schlesinger Library, where they can be pored over to one's heart's content.

Gefilte Fish

- Kosher fish ground up with onions, bread or matzo crumbs, salt, and often potatoes, eggs, and carrots
- Yiddish for "stuffed"
- Originally a European concoction, it became a Jewish menu linchpin by the nineteenth century

For some, gefilte fish calls to mind Mike Myers's affectionate riff on *his* heritage in the film *So I Married an Axe Murderer* that "most Scottish cuisine is based on a dare." Like Scottish haggis, gefilte fish is an acquired taste. It also typically comes in a jar of viscous, jaundiced jelly or a murky sluice that fairly resembles formaldehyde. Gefilte fish fans, meanwhile, can be competitively rigid about the "right way" it should be made and served. Should it be offered with or without horseradish? Should it be sweet or savory? Is it permissible to augment the recipe with corn? All questions whose answers are ultimately subjective. But don't tell *them* that.

> LEARN MORE: For those looking to expand the legacy to the next generation of Jewish gourmands, there's Barbara Cohen's *The Carp in the Bathtub*, published in 1972 and hailed by *Tablet* as "The Greatest Children's Book Ever Written about Gefilte Fish."

Get Critical, Critical[31]

Criticism has been a part of Jewish tradition as far back as Maimonides's[32] critique of the state of Judaism itself, *Commentary on the Mishnah*, published in 1168.

During our modern epoch, Jewish critics have impassionedly tackled everything from food (Jonathan Gold), to gender and sexuality (Judith Butler), to comics (Ariel Dorfman), to corporate power (Naomi Klein), sociopolitics (Glenn Greenwald), media and technology (Neil Postman), the exploration of history (Howard Zinn), the exploration of the future (Alvin Toffler), the act of criticism specifically (Theodor Adorno), and just about *everything* in general (Fran Lebowitz).

Some might call it kvetching. But expert testimony can be of vital assistance.

Here're a few other notable critics:

- **LOTTE EISNER:** bellwether German-French film critic who inspired the revolutionary New Wave of the 1960s and 1970s, which modernized cinema as we know it today
- **TODD GITLIN:** early president of Students for a Democratic Society who penned *The Sixties: Years of Hope, Days of Rage* and *Letters to a Young Activist* before becoming an outspoken critic of the "New Left"
- **CLEMENT GREENBERG:** essential early- to mid-twentieth-century art critic who almost single-handedly popularized painters of the Abstract

31 With apologies to Olivia Newton-John (Jewish on both grandparents' sides, by the way!)
32 Full name Moses ben Maimon, a Sephardic philosopher and religious scholar during the twelfth century

Expressionist school (such as Jackson Pollock and Willem de Kooning), along with the Yiddish word "kitsch" and the French "avant-garde"

- NAT HENTOFF: one of the leading critics of jazz, country, and folk music in the mid-twentieth century
- PAULINE KAEL: standout critic of 1960s–1980s cinema—equally maligned, feared, and beloved by Hollywood insiders; namesake of the villainous General Kael in Ron Howard and George Lucas's *Willow*
- LILLIAN ROXON: in 1959 New York she became a singular voice in the expanding music journalism scene; eventually dubbed "the Mother of Rock"
- GILBERT SELDES: considered to be the first major critic to write about the newly minted category of "Pop Culture" in the early 1900s, Seldes took seriously what his peers thought trivial: comic strips, jazz, cartoons, motion pictures, vaudeville, and Broadway
- GENE SISKEL: affectionately known as half of a two-headed monster of film criticism with lifelong on-screen partner Roger Ebert; the duo *also* inspired an evil creature in *Willow*: the dragon-like Eborsisk
- SUSAN SONTAG: Pop Art (before it was "cool"), Media (before it was a ubiquitous term), monster movies from the 1950s, politics, sexuality, cuisine—Sontag critiqued it all, and even fired off a flaming arrow at *criticism itself*

Girlfriends

- BAFTA/Golden Globe-nominated dramedy
- Ranked among the National Board of Review's top ten films when it premiered in 1978
- Inducted into the Library of Congress's National Film Registry in 2019

Jewish director/co-writer Claudia Weill expanded what was initially a short into *Girlfriends*, the first American independent feature funded by grants. It explores the tempestuous circadian rhythms of twentysomething photographer Susan Weinblatt, who sports big hair, big glasses, and even bigger chutzpah.[33] The cast boasts such Jewish stars as Bob Balaban, Christopher Guest, and Melanie Mayron. This hidden gem prefigured many shows and films about young women making their way in New York City, such as *Sex and the City*, *Girls* (of which Weill was a director), and the Greta Gerwig–starrer *Frances Ha*.

> **LEARN MORE:** Criterion put out the Blu-ray of *Girlfriends* in late 2020, via a box set that includes cast interviews, short films by Weill, and essays by the likes of critic Molly Haskell.

33 Charisma

The Goldbergs

- American family sitcom/soap opera that aired as a radio broadcast from 1929[34] to 1946
- Chronicled the daily goings-on of a "relatively normal" Jewish family in the early twentieth-century Bronx
- One of the most popular broadcasts of radio's Golden Era

"Yoo-hoo!": Here comes Gertrude Berg's Molly Goldberg, the redoubtable matriarch of the Goldberg mishpachah[35] calling out her gregarious catchphrase. Berg created, produced, wrote, directed, and stared in the naturalistic radio program, which became a television show that ran from 1949 to 1956. It would later be adapted into a stage play, film, Broadway musical, and comic strip. As lighthearted as it could be, *The Goldbergs* didn't pull punches when it came to addressing issues of the day, including the Holocaust, the Great Depression, World War II, and anti-Semitism. The Goldbergs kept each other's spirits up through love and laughter, which resonated with the nationwide listenership who each day looked forward to hearing announcer Bud Collyer introduce the one tough macher[36] behind it all: Molly Goldberg.

> LEARN MORE: For further sitcom adventures of a (more modern) "relatively normal" Jewish family, there's Adam Goldberg's *The Wonder Years*–esque *The Goldbergs*.

---

34 First airdate: November 20
35 Family
36 Literally translates to "creator," as in "maker"; influencer/fixer

Goldwater, Barry

- Born January 2, 1909, in Phoenix, Arizona
- Five-term Republican senator for Arizona
- In 1964 became the first candidate of Jewish heritage nominated for president by a major political party

Before there was Bernie Sanders, there was Barry Goldwater. Granted, the two couldn't be any further separated on the political spectrum. But they do share the commonality of being the two candidates of Jewish descent who came closest to becoming President of the United States. In Goldwater's case, he lost to incumbent Democrat Lyndon B. Johnson in one of the greatest landslides in American election history. However, he's largely credited for recalibrating and reigniting the American conservative movement of the era with his book *The Conscience of a Conservative*. Goldwater paved the way for many like-minded politicos—devotees Ronald Reagan and George W. Bush among them—including such Jews as Secretary of State Henry Kissinger and contemporary commentator Ben Shapiro.

LEARN MORE: Goldwater's granddaughter CC appeared on both *The Daily Show* and *Real Time with Bill Maher* to discuss her forebearer's legacy and promote her documentary *Mr. Conservative: Goldwater on Goldwater*, which first premiered on HBO in 2006.

Golem

- Hebrew for "shapeless mass"
- The earliest known instructions for making a golem can be found in the *Sefer Yetzirah* (aka "Book of Creation"), which scholars believe dates back to the Talmudic period (70–640 CE)

The most well-known fable of a golem, a magical humanoid formed of clay and brought to life, centers on sixteenth-century Prague's Rabbi Judah Loew ben Bezalel, who created one to protect his Jewish community and assist with physical labor. Parables of golems often end with the creature running amok and attacking not only its conjurer's enemies but also those it was meant to save. The moral being: *Mere mortals shouldn't dabble in mystically creating life.* This theme has inspired such "modern Prometheus" descendants as *Frankenstein*, *The Island of Dr. Moreau*, *Blade Runner*, *Pet Sematary*, and *Jurassic Park*.

LEARN MORE: *The Simpsons Treehouse of Horror XVII* segment "You Gotta Know When to Golem" features the voices of Jewish comedians Richard Lewis and Fran Drescher. There's also Gustav Meyrink's serialized novel *The Golem*, first published in 1913, which became the inspiration for the 1915 silent film *Der Golem*.

Go on Television

Don't turn that dial on these formidable Jewish TV show masters of the form:

- **SACHA BARON COHEN:** British comedy maven who grew up studying Jewish history and civil rights issues before creating and starring in *Da Ali G Show*, from which he spun off a number of indelible characters such as hapless broadcast journalist Borat Sagdiyev

- **JAMES L. BROOKS:** created, co-created, and/or executive produced *The Mary Tyler Moore Show* and its spin-offs *Rhoda* and *Lou Grant*, as well as *Taxi*, *The Tracey Ullman Show*, and *its* spin-off (of a sort)—*The Simpsons*—and then *its* pseudo-spin-off *The Critic*

- **NAT HIKEN:** journalist-turned-screenwriter-turned-aviator-turned-screenwriter (again) who began writing for early TV icon Milton Berle, became one of Hollywood's first-ever writer-producers, and created Golden Age series *The Phil Silvers Show*[37] and *Car 54, Where Are You?*

- **NORMAN LEAR:** one of the most influential creators in the history of television who, at nearly one hundred years of age, *still* produces for the medium he shaped with such pivotal series as *All in the Family*, *The Jeffersons*, *Maude*, *One Day a Time*, *Sanford and Son*, and *Good Times*

- **DAN LEVY:** scion of comedic multihyphenate Eugene Levy, with whom Dan co-created and starred in the hit sitcom *Schitt's Creek*, a kind of Canadian *Arrested Development* (which was also created by a Jew, Mitchell Hurwitz)

37 Aka *Sgt. Bilko*

- **CHUCK LORRE:** aspiring rock star who tried his hand at writing cartoons before becoming "the King of Sitcoms" for creating/co-creating chart-topping hits including *Grace Under Fire*, *Cybill*, *Dharma & Greg*, *Two and a Half Men*, and *The Big Bang Theory*

- **MICHAEL SCHUR:** former president of the *Harvard Lampoon* who wrote/produced for *SNL* (including the first "Weekend Update" segment after 9/11) and the American iteration of *The Office*, then created/co-created *Parks and Recreation*, *The Good Place*, *Brooklyn Nine-Nine*, and *Rutherford Falls*

- **SHERWOOD SCHWARTZ:** while pursuing his master's degree in biology, Schwartz took a gig penning jokes for Bob Hope's radio program, which led to an illustrious career creating popular sitcoms including *Gilligan's Island* and *The Brady Bunch*

- **ROD SERLING:** *Planet of the Apes* co-writer, political activist, and television wunderkind who created, hosted, and wrote nearly all 156 episodes of the original TV series *The Twilight Zone*

- **JOEY SOLOWAY:** after writing, producing, and showrunning *The Steve Harvey Show*, *Six Feet Under*, and *Grey's Anatomy*, Soloway created Amazon's *Transparent*, which won the first-ever Best Series Golden Globe for a streaming platform and was hailed as "the most Jewish show on television" by *The Guardian* in 2017

Haddish, Tiffany

- Born December 13, 1979, in Los Angeles
- Emmy Award–nominated actress, Grammy Award–winning stand-up comedian, *New York Times* bestselling author, and first Black female stand-up comic to host *SNL*
- Her role as fierce free spirit "Dina" in 2017's *Girls Trip* launched her career into the stratosphere

The only child of a Jewish Ethiopian refugee father and Christian mother, Tiffany Sara Cornilia Haddish has twice been named one of *Hollywood Reporter*'s most influential entertainers. *Time* magazine championed her as one of the most influential people worldwide, *period*. As chronicled in her hilarious but touching memoir *I Curse You with Joy*, Haddish had to use her innate gift for comedy to overcome substantial challenges throughout her foundational years. This included reacquainting with her estranged father at twenty-seven, which led her to rediscover her Jewish identity. When Haddish became a bat mitzvah at age forty, the presiding rabbi at her ceremony was Susan Silverman, sister to fellow femme fatale funnywoman Sarah Silverman.

LEARN MORE: Rediscovering her Jewish roots also inspired Haddish's 2019 Netflix comedy special *Black Mitzvah*. What's more Jewish than sharing a gut-busting laugh while recounting how *fakakta* life can be?

Hamantaschen

- Cream-colored light and buttery cookies bursting at the core with sugary jam flavored by the likes of *mohn*,[38] *powidl*,[39] apricot, or chocolate

- Loosely translates to "Haman's pockets/pouches"—named for the antagonist of Purim
- Inspired by the German *mohntaschen* ("poppyseed pockets")

It was in the sixteenth century that this extremely popular cookie became associated with Purim, a yearly Jewish festival to celebrate the quashing of Haman's plan to exterminate Persian Jews using his position as high political adviser to King Ahasuerus. It's unknown why hamantaschen sport three sides, but one theory is that Haman wore a three-cornered hat. Another is that his allegedly pointy ears were clipped off during his hanging . . . In fact, they are referred to by some Sephardic Jews as *"Orejas de Haman."*[40]

> **LEARN MORE:** Add a dash of history to a whole heap of recipes, and you've got yourself a delectable insight into hamantaschen, courtesy of Joan Nathan's 2017 cookbook *King Solomon's Table: A Culinary Exploration of Jewish Cooking from around the World.*

38 sweetened poppy seed paste
39 unsweetened prune spread
40 ears of Haman

Hatzalah

- Also known as Chevra Hatzalah ("Society of Rescuers")
- The largest nonprofit ambulance service in the United States
- Founded in Williamsburg, Brooklyn, by Rabbi Hershel Weber in 1965

Although Hatzalah specializes in assisting members of the Jewish community worldwide, speaking Yiddish and Hebrew and observing certain religious customs, the organization will serve any person regardless of religion, race, ethnic background, or ability to pay. Funded primarily by private donations, it brings together a network of courageous responders who voluntarily contribute their professional expertise as EMTs, paramedics, physicians, multilingual dispatchers (including Russian, Farsi, Spanish, and French), and general service technicians.

LEARN MORE: For those who want to know more about Hatzalah and potentially get involved in their local branch, there's 2013's user-friendly guidebook *Madrich L'Chevra Hatzalah: A Digest of Halachos Pertaining to Pikuach Nefesh* written by Rabbi Mechel Handler.

Hebrew National Hot Dogs

- Founded in Manhattan's Lower East Side in 1905
- Instead of pork, these kosher hot dogs are made from beef that has been prepared following kashruth[41] law

It's all thanks to Russian immigrant Theodore Krainin, who came to the United States in the 1880s before becoming proprietor of his very own hot dog factory. By 1921, early anti-processed-foods crusader Alfred W. McCann was rhapsodizing that Krainin's dogs well-served New York City's Jewish residents. By 2005, according to the *New York Times*, Hebrew National had become the number one choice for delis and grocery stores carrying kosher hot dogs. It certainly doesn't hurt that their 1965 slogan, "We answer to a higher authority," was identified as one of the longest-running and most well-known marketing campaigns, according to a separate 1997 profile of the company by the *New York Times*.

LEARN MORE: For those interested in a parallel-universe version of Hebrew National hot dogs, the outfit created an offshoot nonkosher brand in 1982 called National Deli. Alas, the "higher authority" didn't seem to be on their side with that one, and the brand was sold off in 2001 . . . to a former Hebrew National employee.

41 Refers to the "laws" of making sure something is kosher

High Holidays

- Also known as the High Holy Days and *Yamim Noraim*, Hebrew for "Days of Awe"
- Take place throughout the month of *Tishrei* (September and October[42])

September and even a bit of October can be an extremely busy time for observant Jews. With the High Holiday season upon them, it's considered a time for such values as resilience, forgiveness, merriment, and liberation. The two primary holidays for this period are Rosh Hashanah[43] (Jewish New Year) and Yom Kippur[44] (Day of Atonement). However, adjacent holidays include Sukkoth, Simchat Torah, and Shemini Atzeret. Whether triumphantly blowing the shofar (ram's horn), fasting, feasting, or otherwise commemorating *Yamim Noraim*, the High Holidays are a time of recognizing we are all as fallible as we are capable of forgiveness—including for ourselves—and renewal. *Shanah tovah!*[45]

LEARN MORE: Reflect further via *Tablet*'s 2021 nine-part podcast series *How to Fix a Soul in 30 Days*, in which host Kylie Unell chronicles her own personal preparation for the High Holidays.

---

42 Depending on how the Jewish/lunisolar calendar coordinates that year with the standard Gregorian calendar
43 Translates to "head of the year"
44 Considered the *holiest* day of the year
45 Hebrew for "Happy new year!"

Highland Park, Chicago

❧ Founded in 1869
❧ Uniquely welcoming to Jewish refugees during World War II, becoming a community stronghold

Of the 300,000 Jews who today live in the Chicago area, 70 percent reside in nearby suburbs such as Highland Park. Though John Hughes's mainstay setting of "Shermer, Illinois" does not exist, the filmmaker used Highland Park for shooting locations in *Ferris Bueller's Day Off*, *Sixteen Candles*, and *Home Alone*. It was also where the films *Risky Business* and *Ordinary People* were shot. Many budding filmmakers were raised here, including writer Steve Zacharias, who co-wrote the *Revenge of the Nerds* franchise. Other notable denizens include Grammy Award–winning Jewish pop-rocker Richard Marx and actress Rachel Brosnahan, who, though not Jewish herself, has attributed her experience growing up here as a source of inspiration when portraying Jewish protagonist "Midge" on *The Marvelous Mrs. Maisel*.

LEARN MORE: Chicago State University Professor Emeritus Irving Cutler, founder of the Chicago Jewish Historical Society, wrote three helpful books published throughout the early 2000s: *The Jews of Chicago: From Shtetl to Suburb*, *Jewish Chicago: A Pictorial History*, and *Chicago's Jewish West Side*.

Hillcrest Country Club

- Founded in 1920 in West Los Angeles
- The area's first such institution to admit Jewish members
- Hosted an informal Friday luncheon attended by the Marx Brothers, George Burns, Jack Benny, and Milton Berle

By 1987, Hillcrest was admitting both non-Jewish and female members. Still, it remains strictly a bastion for the extremely well-to-do. In a 1994 *Cigar Aficionado* interview, Berle quipped, "It cost me $275 to join [in 1932]. Now the initiation fee is $150,000 . . . if they'll accept you, which all depends on how much money you've given to the United Jewish Appeal." After oil was discovered there in the 1950s, Hillcrest memberships became so valuable that they were bequeathed to family members in wills. Initiation fees more or less peaked in 2007 and have plateaued at a manageable $275,000 ever since.

LEARN MORE: As per their website, privacy at Hillcrest is a number one priority. So, don't expect to get into 10000 W. Pico Blvd. for a gander . . . unless you're ready to apply for a membership. Just make sure to bring your required tax returns.

Hora

- Likely originated in the Balkans during the late nineteenth century
- The name has Slavic origins and roughly translates to "round dance"
- Popularized in 1924 by Jewish Romanian choreographer/dancer Baruch Agadati

The hora evolved over decades from participants separated by gender dancing in a circle unattached, to linking their fingers or arms together, to the coed version you may behold today at Jewish celebrations, weddings, and summer camp dances frequently punctuated with a rendition of "Hava Nagila." Paraphrasing Israeli folk dance pioneer Rivka Sturman, the collective intimacy of the hora makes it a dance that is equal parts enthusiastic and egalitarian. Indeed, it's one joyful dance *everyone* can get in on . . . regardless of a lack of rhythm or two left feet.

> LEARN MORE: Documentarian Roberta Grossman produced 2012's *Hava Nagila (The Movie)* in which the history of the traditional song and dance is chronicled and discussed by such celebrity Jews as *Star Trek*'s Leonard Nimoy and alt-rocker Regina Spektor.

How Do I Love Thee?

Some Jewish poets
Here now for you
Some may be familiar
Some may be new

- **HOWARD ASHMAN:** earned two Academy Awards, five Grammys, and wrote the lyrics for rock musical *Little Shop of Horrors* and such Disney songbook mainstays as *The Little Mermaid*, *Beauty and the Beast*, and *Aladdin*
- **ROSEBUD BEN-ONI:** received the 2021 National Jewish Book Award in Poetry for her melding of poetry and science in *If This Is the Age We End Discovery* and has been commissioned by the National September 11 Memorial & Museum
- **LEONARD COHEN:** singer, novelist, and poet best known for exploring styles ranging from lambent folk to hauntingly gothic cabaret
- **ALLEN GINSBERG:** a guiding beacon in the foundational Beat Generation, Ginsberg's 1956 poem "Howl" altered the way poetry would be written, read, and performed from then on
- **HETTIE JONES:** penned a prodigious oeuvre including three collections of poetry and a memoir of her own experience with the Beats
- **EMMA LAZARUS:** activist and writer whose lines from her 1883 sonnet "The New Colossus" are inscribed on a bronze plaque at the base of the Statue of Liberty

- **DOROTHY PARKER:** lethally witty writer specializing in sophisticated wordplay and brutal observations on life and death, who was also the screenwriter for the original *A Star Is Born*
- **AARON SAMUELS:** creator of Blavity, a digital community for Black millennials, with a reported reach of more than one hundred million users; his debut poetry collection *Yarmulkes & Fitted Caps* is acclaimed for promoting the concept of personal identity as an aspirational lifestyle
- **SHEL SILVERSTEIN:** the lyricist behind Johnny Cash's "A Boy Named Sue," who is best known for authoring/illustrating beloved poetry books *The Giving Tree* and *Where the Sidewalk Ends*
- **GERTRUDE STEIN:** a forerunner of the modernist art movement, she hosted from her Paris home a famed salon attended by Ernest Hemingway, Henri Matisse, and F. Scott Fitzgerald

Hum a Few Bars

A list of highly acclaimed, well-remembered, and influential Jewish musical composers could easily fill a book. But, for practicality's sake, here are just a few:

- **IRVING BERLIN:** responsible for more than fifteen thousand songs over six decades, as he put it himself in one of his best-known songs, "There's No Business Like Show Business"
- **LEONARD BERNSTEIN:** recipient of sixteen Grammys, seven Emmys, and the Kennedy Center Honor in 1980
- **GEORGE GERSHWIN:** born at the turn of the twentieth century, he injected the new era's music into the classical idiom, in such hits as "Of Thee I Sing," "Let's Call the Whole Thing Off," and "Rhapsody in Blue"
- **PHILIP GLASS:** brought his heavenly but minimalist operatic style to collaborations with David Bowie, Leonard Cohen, Ravi Shankar, Paul Simon, Linda Ronstadt, Yo-Yo Ma, and others; has also worked with dance choreographer Twyla Tharp, filmmaker Martin Scorsese, and documentarian Errol Morris
- **GYÖRGY LIGETI:** innovator of lush but unsettling orchestral film scores
- **GUSTAV MAHLER:** a leading mind of late nineteenth-century composition who acted as a link between classical music and the modern era; included thrice in *BBC Music Magazine*'s 2016 list of the best symphonies of all time

THE NEWMAN FAMILY: the most Oscar-nominated family in history with paterfamilias Alfred Newman winning nine himself for "Best Original Score"; travel down the family tree to find Thomas Newman (*American Beauty* and *The Shawshank Redemption*), David Newman (*The Mighty Ducks* and *Bill & Ted's Excellent Adventure*), and Newmans: Maria, Emil, Lionel, Jaclyn, Joey, and Randy[46]

ARNOLD SCHOENBERG: pioneered "atonality"[47] as a musical styling (though he was not fond of the term himself); influenced subsequent experimental musicians such as students Anton Webern, John Cage, La Monte Young, and Yoko Ono

STEPHEN SONDHEIM: the lyricist for *West Side Story* and *Gypsy*, Sondheim earned eight Grammys, an Oscar, eight Tonys, a Pulitzer, and a Presidential Medal of Honor

JOHANN STRAUSS: known as "the Waltz King" though long *not* known as a Jew, thanks to Adolf Hitler appropriating such Strauss works as "The Blue Danube" while wiping the composer's heritage from the record

---

46 That final Newman is notable for such beloved rock/pop songs as "I Love L.A." and "You Can Leave Your Hat On"

47 Nontraditional musical style that avoids standard tone, key, or chord patterns

Hummus

- Arabic for "chickpeas"
- Colloquialism for the full name: *ḥummuṣ bi ṭaḥīna* ("chickpeas with tahini")
- First known recipe was recorded in thirteenth-century Egypt

A sepia-colored, smoothly flocculated Middle Eastern puree, hummus is made from cooked, mashed chickpeas, lemon juice, tahini (ground sesame), and garlic. It's perfect for dipping everything from carrots to bell peppers, celery sticks and corn chips. It can be used as a condiment in your gyro or sandwich, and often is by those who are mayonnaise-averse. There are even some who go right in and chomp it down with a spoon, like it was cottage cheese or yogurt. And, yet . . . because of its unknown origins, the "hummus wars" rage on over whether the dish is inherently Israeli or Lebanese. At least there's one thing everyone can agree on: it's *geshmak*.[48]

> **LEARN MORE:** Award-winning Australian documentarian Trevor Graham (whose next film, appropriately enough, would be about mayo) took the aforementioned battle of the bean dip to heart in 2012's intimate but lighthearted *Make Hummus Not War*.

---

48 Yummily tasty

Hydrox Cookies

- Palm-sized, round, dark chocolate cookie sandwich bulging at its center with vanilla cream
- Introduced in 1908, four years earlier than its rival, the Oreo

As per a recent Jewish Telegraphic Agency article, "Hydrox has held on. And at least in part it's because of the Jews." While Oreo went vegetarian in 1997, Hydrox, as they pointed out in a 2021 tweet, has been kosher *since day one*. The "biscuit wars" have been raging since the 1950s when Oreo overtook its predecessor through revolutionary marketing campaigns and a price hike that generated more income for further innovations. Hydrox's parent company Sunshine Biscuits sold off the brand to Keebler in 1996. The cookies were largely discontinued, then purchased and re-released by Leaf Brands in 2015. In 2018, Hydrox filed an $800 million lawsuit with the FTC over what they claimed to be Oreo's unscrupulous anticompetitive practices. Guess that's the way the cookie crumbles.

LEARN MORE: Dunk into award-winning journalist and essayist Jeannette Cooperman's summation told from the perspective of the cookie itself, "Confessions of a Hydrox Cookie."

Improv Comedy

- Short for "improvisational"
- Second City popularized the term "improv comedy" through a new, interactive approach involving audience suggestions

Modern improv comedy melds mid-twentieth-century Method acting developed by Jewish acting theorists and teachers Lee Strasberg, Stella Adler, and Sanford Meisner with theater games originally conceived for therapeutic and communicative use by fellow Jew, Viola Spolin. Spolin's son went on to establish the Compass Players in 1955. Less than five years later, this Chicago-based troupe became the basis for the influential Second City. Jewish icons Harold Ramis, Gilda Radner, Shelley Berman, Mike Nichols, Elaine May, Ed Asner, Alan Arkin, and Jerry Stiller all got their start there. However, the Jewish connection to modern improv extends further, to comedy venues Budd Friedman's The Improv, Mitzi Shore's The Comedy Store, and Jamie Masada's Laugh Factory. It was at such clubs where Andy Kaufman, the Jewish comedian who probably best personifies pure improv comedy, made his mark.

LEARN MORE: Sam Wasson waxes poetic on all things improv comedy in his 2017 extensive history *Improv Nation: How We Made a Great American Art.*

Jewelry Trade

- In 1492 many practicing Jews exiled from Spain found refuge in Antwerp and Amsterdam—known as "the City of Diamonds"
- There, some found work cutting and polishing said diamonds, a role they weren't legally excluded from

Jewelry deals are traditionally closed with a trusting handshake and variant of "mazel tov"—"Mazal and Bracha"[49]—believed to be a tribute to the twelfth-century Jewish scholar Maimonides and his brother David ben Maimon, a dealer of precious stones. And by the late nineteenth century, this trade really took off with the creation of De Beers Consolidated Mines. Founded in part by Jewish brothers Harry and Barney Barnato (né Isaacs), it operated an astonishing 95 percent of the world's diamond industry for a time and remains a leading force in the global diamond trade today.

> LEARN MORE: Shine onto the Jewish Safdie Bros.' 2019 Adam Sandler–starrer *Uncut Gems*, loosely based on anecdotes the filmmaking wunderkinder were told by their father.

49 "Fortune and blessing"

Jewish Community Centers

- Colloquially known as "JCCs"
- Date back to the 1854 founding of Baltimore's Hebrew Young Men's Literary Association
- Merged a century later with the Young Women's Hebrew Association and the Jewish Education Alliance

A lifeline for newly transplanted Jewish immigrants, the first center was established in 1874 in New York City as the Young Men's Hebrew Association, with Lewis May as association president. The name changed to the Jewish Welfare Board in 1917, before the official name of "Jewish Community Centers" was largely adopted in the 1950s. JCCs steadily spread across the United States and Canada, and eventually began welcoming non-Jewish patrons as well. As reported by its own association, these days "JCC professionals reach an estimated two million people annually, including more families with young Jewish children than any group of organizations in North America."

LEARN MORE: As of 2020, there are a recorded 164 JCCs around the country. So, there's a good chance there's one close to you. Go check out what's in store there.

Joyva Candies

- Company founded in 1907 by Nathan Radutzky
- Headquartered in Brooklyn, New York
- Oldest and largest purveyor of halvah

What exactly *is* halvah, anyway? It's not a candy bar. It's not a cracker, nor a cookie. You either can't get enough of it . . . or have to politely ask the person noshing on it nearby to please move *way over there* because of the smell. Ukrainian immigrant Nathan Radutzky was clearly in the former category. He built up what was at first called Independent Halvah & Candies from a humble pushcart. It was in the 1950s that the four Radutzky sons who took over the company came up with the contemporary branding "Joyva." It is a portmanteau of Nathan's granddaughter's name "Roslyn Joy" and, of course, the "halvah" that started it all. Today, descendants of Radutzky run the company, whose line of kashruth candy includes chocolate-covered jelly bars, chocolate-covered marshmallows, and a variety of honey-based Sesame Crunches.

LEARN MORE: Joyva also takes sesame-based grub to another level with its own tahini. Are you courageous enough to taste what happens when a candy company makes seasoned dip that perfectly complements hummus, falafel, and baba ghanoush?

Just One Pant Leg at a Time

Dig that style! Throughout history, Jews have contributed much to the field of sartorial artistry. So turn to the left, and take a gander at these *exemples d'excellence*:

- **MR. GOLDSTEIN:** fictional immigrant tailor in the miniseries *Roots: The Next Generation* who represents the Jewish merchants of the post–Civil War South who did their best to clothe their fellow townspeople . . . despite being set upon by the era's entrenched anti-Semitism that could result (as it did for Goldstein) in harassment, vandalism, and destruction of store and home

- **EDITH HEAD:** winner of a record-breaking eight Academy Awards for Best Costume Design from 1949 to 1973, making her the most Oscar-earning woman of all time; immortalized for her unique style of large black sunglasses and short bobbed black hair as spotlighted by "Edna Mode" in Pixar's *The Incredibles*

- **MARC JACOBS:** toast of the late 1980s glitterati for infusing a youthful "punk" aesthetic into his line of high-fashion garments, he later became creative director for Louis Vuitton and was listed in 2010 as one of *Time* magazine's most influential one hundred people on the planet

- **CALVIN KLEIN:** established Calvin Klein Inc. in 1968 before his name became synonymous[50] with the multitude of designer fashion and fragrance wares his company produces and distributes

---

50 As exhibited in 1985's *Back to the Future*, when protagonist Marty McFly is mistaken for "Calvin Klein" due to the label on his designer purple underwear seen by his future mother Lorraine

ESTÉE LAUDER: Josephine Esther Mentzer gained interest in retail at the family hardware store, learned about cosmetics from her chemist uncle, then started the cosmetics company bearing her name in 1946

RALPH LAUREN: born Ralph Lifshitz, this billionaire designer grew up in the same Bronx community as Calvin Klein and started off in 1967 in the modest realm of ties, the first of his eponymous lines

ISAAC MIZRAHI: given his first sewing machine at ten, started his own clothing line at fifteen, and is known today as fashion designer, television personality, and former head judge on *Project Runway All Stars*

RELIGIOUS RAIMENT: there's the cloth or silk yarmulke,[51] most commonly worn by observant Jewish men in the tradition of keeping one's head covered as humble tribute to the Creator; some women might wear sheitels (wigs) or *tichels* (headscarves); there's also the tallith, a fringed prayer shawl; and the kittel, a knee-length cloth robe donned by those conducting spiritual ceremonies such as Passover

LEVI STRAUSS: German immigrant who started San Francisco–based Levi Strauss & Co.[52] in 1853 selling dry goods during the heyday of the Gold Rush, and in 1873 partnered with Latvian-born fellow Jew Jacob W. Davis[53] to become history's first manufacturer of blue jeans

---

51 Also known as a kippah or skullcap
52 aka Levi's
53 Born Jākobs Jufess, he was the inventor while Strauss was the mass-producer/distributor

Kabbalah

- From the Rabbinical Hebrew *qabbālāh*—originally stemming from the Latin medieval *cabala/cabbala*—and translating to "tradition"
- A vein of Jewish mysticism whose most significant series of texts is called the Zohar
- Historians date kabbalah back to the twelfth and thirteenth centuries

In looking for a connection between this ontological branch and modern practice, look no further than sixteenth-century rabbi, poet, and kabbalist Rabbi Shlomo ha-Levi Alkabetz, who penned the "L'cha Dodi," a hymn used in part to usher in Shabbat that today remains an integral aspect of the holy day. Or to German-born Israeli philosopher Gershom Scholem, who in a series of lectures and writings throughout the mid-twentieth century, described kabbalah as all about "the tradition of the things divine." It was Scholem who, the *New Yorker* suggested in a March 2017 remembrance, "single-handedly turned an obscure theological tradition into a formal discipline, and challenged academia itself with a lush, alien spirituality."

LEARN MORE: Take an intimately personal journey into the realm of Kabbalah in documentarian Steven Bram's 2014 film *Kabbalah Me*. There's also Rabbi Yisroel Bernath's *Kabbalah for Everyone* podcast, which may be of some assistance for the neophyte curious about what the heck it all means.

Kafka, Franz

- Born July 3, 1883, in Prague
- Towering figure of twentieth-century literature
- Best known for his absurdist 1915 novella *The Metamorphosis*

Though the vast majority of his work was published posthumously, Kafka influenced future writers with his canny ability to seamlessly fuse humor with horror, insight with absurdity, and dire angst with a certain luminous playfulness. Kafka succumbed to his lifelong bout with tuberculosis at the age of forty, believing in the end that he was a failure. This proved to be untrue, however—as seen years later through the publication and promotion of his work by friend, fellow writer, and literary executor Max Brod.[54] Kafka's oeuvre has even inspired a neologistic, often hard-to-define literary style called "Kafkaesque": an approach that evokes bewilderment at the faceless indifference of modern society's relentless bureaucracy. Can be pretty funny in the right hands. Like Kafka's.

> **LEARN MORE:** It's all right there in the complete diaries of Franz Kafka (1910–1923), published in 1964.

---

54 Who famously ignored Kafka's final wish of *burning/destroying* said work

Kaifeng, China

- One of the Eight Ancient Capitals of China
- Home to China's oldest surviving Jewish community
- A Ming Dynasty (1368–1644) emperor categorized Kaifeng Jews into eight family names still in use today: Ai, Shi, Gao, Gan, Jin, Li, Zhang, and Zhao

Experts have long debated how Judaism ended up in China. Did practitioners arrive by land over the Silk Road? Were they refugees escaping the horrors of the Crusades? Were they migrating from Persia or India? Or perhaps Iraq? Were they predominantly Mizrahi (Western Asian/North African) . . . or Bukharan (exiled by the Babylonians from current-day Israel)? Though it's now believed Jews first arrived between the seventh and twelfth centuries, it wasn't until 1605 that Europeans even realized such a community existed in China. Although discoverer Jesuit priest Matteo Ricci's conversion attempts were rebuffed, the Kaifeng community did ask if he'd be their rabbi. Perhaps a pork lover, Ricci declined.

LEARN MORE: Written works on the complex story of Kaifeng Jews include Hebrew and Chinese scholar Tiberiu Weisz's *The Kaifeng Stone Inscriptions* and Fook-Kong Wong's *The Haggadah of the Kaifeng Jews of China*. For documentaries, you have a choice of at least four: *Kaifeng, Jerusalem*; *Legacy*; *Quest for the Lost Tribes*; and *Minyan in Kaifeng*.

Kibbutz

- From the Hebrew word *qibbus* ("gathering")
- The first kibbutz was founded in 1909
- With nearly three hundred operating throughout Israel today, less than a third remain truly communal

The original notion of a kibbutz can be considered a utopian one: pooling earned income for equally shared monthly stipends within an Israeli-based agrarian community. The movement peaked in the late 1980s, and as of 2016 there were fewer than 150,000 kibbutzniks[55] nationwide. Many such communes have become privatized. As Shimrit Barzily, marketing manager of Kibbutz Ein Gev, explained to *i* newspaper in March 2022, "Kibbutzim these days aren't just farming collectives; they have all kinds of businesses—from food processing to electronics." It's worth noting that Ein Gev, established in the 1930s, now runs its own four-star holiday resort, gourmet fish restaurant, and 2,500-seat concert venue. That's a modern-day kibbutz for you.

> **LEARN MORE:** Explore more of the kibbutz story in the 2008 documentary *Degania: The First Kibbutz Fights Its Last Battle*, or the 2011 Israeli miniseries *Barefoot*—which follows three generations of kibbutzim in a fictionalized depiction of the complex lifestyle.

55 Member of a kibbutz

Klezmer Music

- Yiddish name can be translated as "vessel of song"
- Traditional instruments include fiddle, bass, cello, clarinet, drum, accordion and/or hammered dulcimer
- Incorporates elements of Eastern European folk, Roma, and French café/early jazz music

Originating in the 1400s, klezmer became so popular in Jewish circles that by the 1800s, the genre had become synonymous with "musician" and "instrumentalist." It often attempts to emulate the emotional resonance of weeping, laughing, and, via the violin player, a cantor's[56] singing. Klezmer can be so infectiously jubilant that it may lead to a rash of dancing waltzes, polkas, and tangos. After its popularity dwindled during World War II, there was a buoyant resurgence in the 1970s. NYU professor Barbara Kirshenblatt-Gimblett writes about this as the "Klezmer Revival," a period marked by the frequent joining of forces between klezmer and the likes of modern jazz and punk.

LEARN MORE: Aside from paragons such as the *Fiddler on the Roof* soundtrack and the compilation *Yiddish-American Klezmer Music (1925–1956)*, there's *plenty* of klezmer music in just about *any* comedic or romantic movie made by just about *any* Jewish filmmaker during the 1970s and 1980s.

---

56 Guide for singing and orating prayers during religious ceremonies

Knish

- Roundish, decadently buttery, and flaky bun stuffed with savory fillings
- The word itself is the Yiddish etymological descendant of the Ukrainian *knysh* and Polish *knysz*, a medieval-era fried vegetable patty

Filled with mashed potatoes, cheese, spinach, or mushrooms, before they're fried or baked to a varnished golden brown, knishes are today a recognizable street vendor staple in New York City. But the first American knishery was Yonah Schimmel's Knish Bakery, established in 1910, and identified in a recent *Times of Israel* feature as "one of the last distinctly Jewish businesses in the Lower East Side." In the past, so crucial was a demonstrable passion for knishes that, as per Milton Glaser and Jerome Snyder's 1967 foodie guide *The Underground Gourmet*, "No New York politician in the last 50 years has been elected to office without having at least one photograph showing him on the Lower East Side with a knish in his face."

LEARN MORE: *Whatever Works* from 2009 features Jewish duo Larry David and Evan Rachel Wood's on-screen kooky knish-ery in none other than Yonnah Schimmel's.

Kochi, India

❧ Long nicknamed "the Queen of the Arabian Sea"
❧ A nexus point for the Indian spice trade
❧ Hosts the oldest community of Jews in India, dating back to King Solomon's reign (970–931 BCE)

Originally known in English as "Cochin," and frequently called "Ernakulam," Kochi was long a meeting point for enterprising Chinese, Greek, Jewish, Roman, and Syrian traders. In the fifteenth century, the Kochinim were joined by some of the Iberian Jews exiled by the Spanish monarchy. These "newcomers" became known by locals as Paradesi, aka *Foreign* Jews. India became independent from British rule a year before Israel became recognized as a sovereign state. It was then that the Jews of Kochi began to make aliyah.[57] Some also emigrated to British Commonwealth territories and the United States. Today the Jewish community in Kochi is quite small, but its nearly five-hundred-year-old Paradesi Synagogue remains active.

LEARN MORE: Historical analyses include Nathan Katz and Ellen S. Goldberg's *The Last Jews of Cochin*, as well as 1995 autobiography *Ruby of Cochin* by Ruby Daniel—the first female Kochinim to pen such a chronicle.

57 Similar to the Muslim hajj, this is a spiritual tradition of leaving the so-called "diaspora" for what observant Jews believe to be their Holy Land of Israel

Krav Maga

- Hebrew for "combat contact"
- Originated in the mid- to late 1930s by Hungarian martial artist Imi Lichtenfeld
- First used to counter the rise of fascist aggression in the Jewish quarter of Bratislava, Czechoslovakia

This hybrid defensive and fighting system developed by the Israeli military combines elements of aikido, boxing, judo, karate, and wrestling. And similar to these martial arts on which it's based, Krav Maga's primary directive is to first *avoid* confrontation altogether. *But . . .* if you *do* find yourself in an unavoidable fight, well . . . proponents of the form believe the best way to handle it is *fast* and *efficaciously*, similar to *Kill Bill*'s fictional Five Point Palm Exploding Heart Technique. That's why Krav Maga teaches instinctive attacks on the most vulnerable points of an opponent's body with no regard for avoidance of serious injury or even death. It's this lack of rules or compassion for one's opponent that disqualifies it from sports status. After creator Lichtenfeld passed away in 1998, his protégé, Haim Gidon, spun off his own approved iteration: the Gidon System.

LEARN MORE: There are plenty of guidebooks on the various, ever-changing techniques of Krav Maga.

Kreplach

- Doughy, often wet and slippery Jewish boiled dumplings filled with potatoes or chopped meat; frequently served as part of a chicken soup or as a fried appetizer or side dish
- Regularly served during ceremonial meals on such Jewish holy days as Yom Kippur, Rosh Hashanah, and (usually with vegetarian or dairy-based filling) Purim

As pointed out by an August 2018 *Pittsburgh Jewish Chronicle* feature, kreplach's original appearance in the Jewish community may have been a product of the "stuffed pasta" concept migrating from Italy to Jews in Germany during the thirteenth century. A more modern tradition dictates that each family or chef creates their kreplach in a characteristic shape almost like a family crest. But, in the end, regardless of shape, "Kreplach is kreplach," as summed up by chef Cheryl Blumenfeld in the same *Jewish Chronicle* article. "It all came down from someone's grandparents."

LEARN MORE: Hear all about the perfectly pillowy kreplach in the OJA (Ontario Jewish Archives) Podcast episode "The Humble Kreplach" as hosted by OJA archivist Faye Blum. And for a bit more of the story *and* some tasty recipes, there's Carol Ungar's 2015 illustrated cookbook *Jewish Soul Food: Traditional Fare and What It Means*.

Krusty the Clown

- Voiced by *The Simpsons* series regular Dan Castellaneta
- Though his image appears in earlier episodes, Krusty's first speaking part on *The Simpsons* was 1990's "The Telltale Head"

Full name Sir Herschel Shmoikel Pinchas Yerucham Krustofsky, Krusty is the host of his own long-running televised variety program within *The Simpsons* universe. He was initially based on creator Matt Groening's childhood local TV clown Rusty Nails. Krusty has blossomed over the decades into a kaleidoscopic spectrum of vintage Jewish comedians, such as Milton Berle, Sid Caesar, and Joan Rivers. Off camera, Krusty is a hard-living depressive who is equally boastful and self-deprecatory (often boasting *about* his self-deprecation). Despite his wealth and fame, Krusty struggles with the estrangement from his late father, Rabbi Hyman Krustofsky, voiced by Jackie Mason. Rabbi Krustofsky wanted his son to follow in his footsteps. Krusty chose a life of clowning instead.

LEARN MORE: Insider information about this pathetic *pagliaccio* can be found in Mike Reiss's memoir *Springfield Confidential*. As one of two *Simpsons* writers on staff since its series premiere, Reiss provides expert testimony about the character. Surprising tidbits include how Krusty led to the creation of fellow animated Jewish TV host Jay Sherman on late-nineties cult classic *The Critic*.

Latkes

- Yiddish for "little pancake"
- Originally prepared with deep-fried ricotta cheese, then with *grain* in the fourteenth-century Italian Jewish community
- Ceremonially served during Chanukah due to its celebratory use of oil

The potato-based approach was a nineteenth-century innovation. And why the heck not? As the *New York Times'* Joan Nathan notes in a 2015 column, these fried potato fritters are "traditional, nostalgic, and crispy." There's even a classic Yiddish song to hurrah both Chanukah and latke-eating, written by Jewish Lithuanian Mordkhe Rivesman, and translated into English in 1911. There's no one agreed-upon recipe for the perfect latke. Should the potato be shredded or mashed? How thick should the pancake be? Everyone has their own traditions and preferences, but as long as there's potato and it's fried, you can't really go wrong.

LEARN MORE: The long-running debate about what Jewish food should be the ultimate Purim dish has made for an omnibus of scholarly essays published in 2006 and appropriately titled *The Great Latke-Hamantash Debate* curated by editor Ruth Fredman Cernea.

"Live Long and Prosper"

- Jewish blessing synonymous with Commander S'Chn T'Gai Spock's "Vulcan salute"
- Debuted in *Star Trek*'s second-season premiere: September 15, 1967
- First spoken in Vulcan in 1979's *Star Trek: The Motion Picture* as "*Dif-tor heh smusma*"

The saying was likely borrowed from Deuteronomy 5:33's "so that you may live and prosper." *Star Trek* creator Gene Roddenberry granted Nimoy free rein to embrace his Jewish heritage, which led Nimoy to pair the words of the salute with the *Cohanim* hand gesture. The *original* blessing is traditionally accompanied by a two-hand version while the congregation *looks away*. But, folks, c'mon: *It's a TV show.*

LEARN MORE: If ever you're in Ontario, Canada, pop into Beth Emeth Bais Yehuda Synagogue where Rabbi Howard Morrison, a self-proclaimed expert of nerd TV culture may wax scholarly on all things *Trek* and its intersection with Jewish culture, including fellow Jews William "Captain Kirk" Shatner, Walter "Chekov" Koenig, and Arlene Martel, the actress who played Spock's betrothed in the episode where the salute was first used, "Amok Time."

Lox

- Usually, but not necessarily, smoked and *always* brined fillet of salmon, often served with cream cheese, purple onion, tomato, cucumbers, and pickled capers on a bagel
- From the Yiddish *laks* that, originating in 1940, essentially means "salmon"
- Name is an etymological descendant of the Middle/Old High German *lahs*, the Old English *leax*, and the Old Norse *lax*, related to the Scandinavian "gravlax"

Since arriving in the United States from Eastern Europe in the nineteenth century, lox has been updated from its potently briny, salty origins and is these days often served "Nova" style[58]—*lightly* salted and, yes, *smoked*. It is often used as a topper for a salmon Benedict: lightly toasted bagel/bread upon which one lays silkily thin lox, blanketed in a drippily decadent poached egg, creamily tangy hollandaise sauce, and garnished with dill. A highly variable cut of salmon, it works well in scrambled eggs, omelets, and even as a platter all its own: *lox, stock, and barrel.*

> LEARN MORE: Take a big ol' bite out of the fourth episode of the podcast *Year of the Sandwich*: "The Open-Faced Lox Sandwich and 'Is Bacon as Kosher as Christmas?'"

---

58 As in "Nova Scotia"

Mah-Jongg

- Tile-based parlor game developed in nineteenth-century China
- Brought to the United States in 1912 by a Standard Oil representative
- The first sets were sold in the United States by Abercrombie & Fitch

Historian Annelise Heinz's 2021 book *Mahjong: A Chinese Game and the Making of Modern American Culture* tracks the popularity of the game over time, shedding light on the Jewish women behind the formation of the National Mah Jongg League in 1938. She goes on to describe how, by the 1960s, the game became "a way of building new social networks," particularly as Jewish American families migrated away from urban centers toward suburban areas where they often felt isolated. Heinz is optimistic about the game's future, believing new players will come to it as a "way to connect with their Jewish identities and rekindle memories of their mothers."

LEARN MORE: There's the 1998 documentary *Mah-Jongg: The Tiles That Bind* for those who want to *see* firsthand how the game is played and why it's become such a social epoxy for Chinese and Jewish players alike.

Making Sure to Remember

Though it can feel impossible, reckoning with the facts of the Holocaust is a fundamental consideration of today's Jewish identity. Many notable literary and cinematic works remind us to "never forget."

- *THE BELLAROSA CONNECTION:* 1989 novel structured as a lengthy discourse among a family regarding the impact of the Holocaust on their modern-day lives by Saul Bellow, the only writer to win the National Book Award for Fiction three times
- *THE DIARY OF A YOUNG GIRL:* there is no more meticulously detailed recollection of how the Holocaust impacted average Jewish families than this piercingly intimate exploration of teenage Anne Frank's inner thoughts as recounted in her private journal
- *JOJO RABBIT:* 2019 Academy Award–winning dramedy from Jewish director/writer Taika Waititi, who was inspired by stories of his grandfather fighting Nazis to adapt Christine Leunens's novel about a young Hitler Youth member navigating an existential crisis over his government's "Final Solution"
- *THE LAST CYCLIST:* satirical play penned in cabaret style by young Czech playwright Karel Švenk, created and rehearsed with fellow captured Jews while interned in the Terezin concentration camp

LIFE IS BEAUTIFUL: 1997's multiple Oscar-winning film written and directed by Roberto Benigni, who also stars as a parent going to extreme lengths to keep up his young son's spirits while both are interned in a concentration camp

MAUS: the first (and *only*) graphic novel to win the Pulitzer Prize; a striking visual representation of underground comix icon Art Spiegelman's father's memories of the Holocaust

NIGHT: first published in Yiddish as *Un di Velt Hot Geshvign*[59] in 1956 as Nobel laureate Elie Wiesel's reflections on his coming-of-age in concentration camps while caring for his ailing father

NUMBER THE STARS: winner of both 1990's Newberry Medal and National Jewish Book Award (Children's Literature), this historical novel tells the harrowing story of a ten-year-old Danish girl's flight from Nazi occupation; author Lois Lowry based her work in part on interviews she personally conducted

SCHINDLER'S LIST: 1993 Academy Award–sweeping film based on Thomas Keneally's 1982 historical fiction *Schindler's Ark*, which tells the story of how German industrial magnate Oskar Schindler employed, and thus rescued, nearly 1,500 Jewish refugees in his factories

SHOAH: it took over a decade for French director Claude Lanzmann to produce this nearly ten-hour documentary whose title means "calamity" and "destruction" in Hebrew

59 *And the World Remained Silent*

Manischewitz Wine

- Namesake parent company was founded by Lithuanian American Rabbi Dov Behr Manischewitz in 1888
- Known as Cincinnati's B. Manischewitz Company, they came on the scene originally as innovators of the first-ever mass production of matzo
- Currently one of the largest worldwide producers of kashruth wine

"Man-O-Manischewitz! What a Wine!" is the slogan long promoted by the purveyors of this sweet, sweet *vayn*.[60] The clarion call evidently resonated across the cultural spectrum quickly after it was fermented and distributed en masse once Prohibition was repealed in 1933. As indicated in a 1954 analysis by *Commentary* (founded a decade earlier by an all-Jewish committee), sales of Manischewitz drastically rose during such non-Jewish holidays as Thanksgiving, Christmas, and even St. Patrick's Day. Today, Manischewitz is America's number one kosher wine. Of course, it also remains an essential element of the kiddush, a blessing recited during Shabbat and other holy days.

> **LEARN MORE:** Jewish culinary chronicler Roger Horowitz dives deep into the vat of Manischewitz history throughout the pages of 2016's *Kosher USA: How Coke Became Kosher and Other Tales of Modern Food.*

---

60 You guessed it: *wine*

The Marx Bros.

- Early twentieth-century comedy troupe made up of five[61] brothers: Chico (Leonard), Harpo (Adolph then Arthur), Groucho (Julius), Gummo (Milton), and Zeppo (Herbert)
- Their films were often written in part by some of the era's glitteriest Jewish literary stars, such as George S. Kaufman and S. J. Perelman

The Bros. created such landmark pictures as *Animal Crackers*, *Duck Soup*, *Horse Feathers*, *Monkey Business*, and *A Night at the Opera*. During the Great Depression, there was no shortage of people who would use the few cents they could barely squeeze together for food to pop into a theater to see the latest Marx Bros. film. *That's* how much people during that time needed a laugh and brief sense of collective bonhomie, courtesy of a few very fast-thinking, high-flying, artistic innovators of modern comedy.

LEARN MORE: Laughs and insights can be found in Harpo's 1961 autobiography *Harpo Speaks!*, Steve Stoliar's 1996 memoir *Raised Eyebrows: My Years Inside Groucho's House*, and Robert Weide's definitive 1982 documentary *The Marx Brothers in a Nutshell*.

61 There were technically *six*, but the first—Manfred—passed away in infancy

Matlin, Marlee

- Born August 21, 1965, in Morton Grove, Illinois
- The first Deaf performer and youngest Best Actress to win an Oscar
- Known for roles in such films as 1986's *Children of a Lesser God* and 2021's *CODA*

Growing up in a Reform Jewish household, Matlin attended Congregation Bene Shalom—a synagogue for the Deaf. Matlin became a bat mitzvah after learning her Hebrew prayers phonetically. She began performing publicly at age seven and was later discovered by fellow Jewish performer—the Fonz himself—Henry Winkler, at whose home she was married in 1993. Matlin is extremely active in charitable and humanitarian causes for both her Deaf and Jewish communities. She also possesses an indefatigable sense of humor about her deafness, as she exhibits as guest star on such high-profile comedy series as *Family Guy* and *The Larry Sanders Show.*

LEARN MORE: There's Marlee Matlin's 2010 autobiography *I'll Scream Later*, which delves deep into the actress's well-known humor, as well as her passion for her art. And the *Hollywood Reporter*'s podcast series *Hollywood Remixed* includes Matlin, and her longtime ASL interpreter Jack Jason, on the August 2021 episode "Amplifying Deaf Representation."

Matzo

~ From the Hebrew *maṣṣā* ("juiceless") and Yiddish *matse* or *matzoh* ("unleavened[62] bread")

~ Served ceremonially during the week of Passover, as a reminder of how thirteenth-century BCE Jews fled from Egyptian enslavement in such haste they couldn't even wait for their dough to rise before packing their supplies

Whether served as is, complemented with a spreadable schmear, or mashed up while still in the dough phase as a ball to be served in a hearty chicken soup, matzo must be one of the most versatile and enduring of Jewish cuisine staples. Interestingly, there exists nonkosher matzo . . . for reasons no one can really understand. For matzo to be truly kashruth, it must be produced in less than eighteen minutes from when the instant water meets the flour to the moment it's taken from the oven, in order to assure there's *no* leavening whatsoever. This means specialized equipment, production/cleaning protocol, and a rabbinical supervisory team. Amazing that something so seemingly simple can be one heck of a crunch to produce.

LEARN MORE: Three words: *A Rugrats Passover.*

---

62 Sans yeast or other leavening agent

Milk, Harvey

- Born May 22, 1930, in Woodmere, New York
- Elected as San Francisco city supervisor in 1977
- The first nonincumbent openly gay man to hold public office in the United States

Dubbed the honorary "Mayor of Castro Street,"[63] Harvey Milk was an immensely beloved activist and organizer not just in the neighborhood where he lived and ran a camera store but also within the larger gay rights movement of the 1970s. After taking office, Milk was assassinated by former city supervisor Dan White. And yet, during his eleven months as an elected official, Milk was able to effect dramatic changes in how San Francisco ran. From making sure that people would be fined if they neglected to pick up after their dog, to sponsoring a glass ceiling–shattering nondiscrimination bill, Milk is today considered a visionary by the many he inspired to fight for what they believe in.

LEARN MORE: There's 1984's Academy Award winner for Best Documentary Feature, *The Life and Times of Harvey Milk*; Gus Van Sant's 2008 feature film *Milk*; and 1982's *The Mayor of Castro Street*, written by Randy Shilts. There's also a Harvey Milk opera, children's book, and French YA novel.

63 It's possible Milk awarded himself that encomium, but in all fairness: *it stuck*

Mount Sinai Beth Israel Hospital

- Teaching hospital in Manhattan's Lower East Side
- The Beth Israel Hospital Association formed in 1889

Beth Israel was first incorporated nearly a century ago by forty Orthodox Jews fleeing Russian persecution, each contributing twenty-five cents ($789.85 by 2022 standards). The aim was to establish a hospital to serve Jewish immigrants in LES tenement slums, for whom it was nearly impossible to find a medical facility that would tend to them, due to the era's pervasive anti-Semitism. However, even *it* could barely suffice, with only twenty-eight beds. By 1965, the institution had purchased neighboring Manhattan General, renamed it "Beth Israel Hospital," and served all patients regardless of religious affiliation. A series of similar acquirements, relocations, and name changes followed. On November 22, 2013, after another such merger, a new name was decided on: "Mount Sinai Beth Israel." Beth Israel ceased operating its kosher kitchen as of December 2015. But it does still sport a synagogue.

LEARN MORE: New York City's James Joseph Walsh was a medical practitioner *and* historian who chronicled the city's burgeoning health industry. This included entries about Beth Israel and its sister organizations in his five-volume *History of Medicine in New York: Three Centuries of Medical Progress*, published in 1919. Slightly less daunting, there's also Beth Israel's website.

Museum of Tolerance

- Established in 1993 as the educational branch of the Los Angeles–based Simon Wiesenthal[64] Center
- Has received over five million visitors
- In addition to its exploration of worldwide anti-Semitism, the museum engages patrons, including many middle and high school students, in investigations of other global atrocities as well as acts of everyday bullying

As difficult as it can be to come face-to-face with interactive multimedia exhibits and direct evidence displaying some of the worst tragedies of human civilization—particularly the Holocaust—the Museum of Tolerance (MOT) remains a comprehensive repository of all-ages hands-on research in order for those participating to better understand not only these horrendous historical events . . . but human nature *itself*, and its capacity for both great evil and great compassion. It is MOT's mission and hope that such primary instruction will inspire positive acts or mitzvoth by patrons who visit it.

LEARN MORE: The 2007 film *Freedom Writers*, which is based on a true story, features a lengthy sequence at the MOT.

---

64 Notable Holocaust survivor and Nazi hunter who approved of his name being so used but was not directly involved in operations

Pejsachówka

- Brandy made from fermented damascene (damson plum)
- A popular Kosher spirit imbibed on Passover, with the Polish *"pejsachówka"* stemming from Pesach, the Hebrew word for the holiday
- Alternative names and spellings include: Schlivowitz, slivovice, slivovica—and *raika* in the Balkans, *țuică* in Romania, *pálenka* in Ukraine, or *pălincă* in Greece and Italy

Pejsachówka—or in its less colloquial iteration, slivovitz—isn't merely beloved by pious Jews who can't drink beer or bourbon during Passover.[65] Slivovitz was in fact *so* popular among various European traditions that a minor cold war was waged over its national provenance. The European Union stepped up to broker a compromise in 2007. No fewer than fifteen countries were granted the right of "Protected Designation of Origin" over slivovitz . . . as long as they use their own distinctive word to describe it—hence the many, *many* variations aforementioned.

> **LEARN MORE:** Bear witness to what a whole Herculean heaping of slivovitz does to someone in Terry Zwigoff's film *Art School Confidential*. College art students repeatedly ply a former alumnus-turned-wastrel with a bottle of 80-proof *pejsachówka* to gain admittance to his cluttered, rent-controlled sanctum.

65 Many liquors are brewed with grain, which makes them not kosher for Passover

Perlman, Itzhak

- Born August 31, 1945, in Tel Aviv
- Has won sixteen Grammys, four Emmys, and received the Presidential Medal of Freedom in 2015 from President Barack Obama, at whose 2009 inauguration Perlman performed

Virtuoso Israeli American violinist Itzhak Perlman contracted polio at age four, which left him in lifelong need of leg braces and crutches. But as he told NPR in 2015, "I'm not onstage to do walking. I'm on the stage to play." And play Perlman has. After being denied admittance by the first conservatory he applied to for being too small to hold the violin (he was *three*), Perlman taught *himself* to handle the instrument. He reapplied to conservatory, was accepted, had his first recital at ten, and moved to the United States, where he became a thirteen-year-old Juilliard prodigy. He concurrently debuted his talent to the world at large on *The Ed Sullivan Show*. Perlman returned six years later in the same episode that introduced the world to *another* everlasting musical icon: the Rolling Stones.

LEARN MORE: In 2017, award-winning documentarian Alison Chernick released *Itzhak*, her in-depth film on the life, times, and religious heritage of Perlman. Or enjoy your fill of his music through the 2015 seven-disc box set *Itzhak Perlman: The Complete Warner Recordings*.

Pikesville, Baltimore

- Baltimore's Lloyd Street Synagogue is the third-oldest standing temple nationwide
- Contains one of the largest Jewish populations throughout the State of Maryland
- Notable resident and internet celebrity Sam Barsky specializes in clothes that playfully showcase Jewish iconography

Though it's a mere twelve square miles in size, Pikesville is home to *two* kosher grocery stores, of which one—Seven Mile Market—remains among the country's largest. In the nineteenth and early twentieth centuries, Baltimore became a welcoming port for Jewish immigrants seeking their fortune in the New World. After World War II, Jewish Baltimoreans tiring of big-city life moved to the nearby slower-paced and *haimish*[66] Pikesville. This exodus escalated in the late 1960s as a consequence of turmoil resulting from the Vietnam War and civil unrest roiling Baltimore proper.

LEARN MORE: Pikesville is less than five miles from the *Baltimore Jewish Times*, one of the oldest operational Jewish newspapers in the United States. A deeper investigation of the area's Jewish history is thus a mere microfiche session away.

66 Cozy, unpretentious, friendly

Portnoy's Complaint

- Authored by Philip Roth, who lived 1933–2018
- Published by Random House on January 12, 1969
- Kick-started Roth's prodigiously prolific career

Roth incorporated many intimate motifs reminiscent of his own emotional life in penning the bildungsroman of protagonist Alexander Portnoy. The story focuses on Portnoy's humorously awkward sexual awakening as recounted during a rambling therapy session. Think of it as a Jewish counterpart to a Catholic confessional . . . with creative onanistic machinations. Indeed, due to its compulsive fixation on masturbation, mothers, and meshuggaas, Roth's novel is considered a quintessential work of Jewish male neuroticism. It has since become a catchphrase for the affliction captured on its first page: "A disorder in which strongly-felt ethical and altruistic impulses are perpetually warring with extreme sexual longings, often of a perverse nature."

LEARN MORE: The novel earned a spot on both *Time* magazine's "100 Best English-Language Novels from 1923 to 2005" and the Modern Library's "100 Best English-Language Novels of the 20th Century." And yet, the 1972 film adaptation was resoundingly considered by esteemed critics to be an embarrassing misfire on all fronts.

Raz, Lior

- Co-creator and star of Netflix's *Fauda*, based on Raz's and creative partner Avi Issacharoff's experiences serving in the IDF[67] special forces unit
- After airing in 2015, *Fauda* won six Ophirs (the Israeli equivalent of the Emmy Awards), including Best Drama

Raz was born and grew up in Ma'ale Adumim, a small town only a few miles from Jerusalem, after his parents settled there from their respective homelands of Algeria and Iraq. Raz was raised speaking both Hebrew and Arabic. In 1993, he left for the United States, where his military background secured him employment as a personal bodyguard for none other than Arnold Schwarzenegger. Raz later returned to Israel, attended Tel Aviv's Nissan Nativ Drama School, began acting, and landed a featured role in Chris Weitz's 2018 historical drama *Operation Finale*, alongside Ben Kingsley, Nick Kroll, and Oscar Isaac.

> LEARN MORE: Although it ends with a cliffhanger, Netflix canceled Raz and Issacharoff's next series, 2021's *Hit & Run*, after one season. But it's out there if you want to see more Lior Raz in action.

---

67 Israeli Defense Forces, Israel's combined military branches

Ready, Set, Score!

There's a long-standing history of sportsmanship in Jewish culture. Exhibit the Maccabiah Games, the third-largest sporting event worldwide,[68] established in 1932 as a multi-sport Jewish Olympics of sorts held once every four years in Israel. When it comes to listing favorite athletes, don't bench the Jewish players in your bracket without considering:

- **MAX BAER:** world heavyweight championship boxer, referee, disc jockey, wrestler, and actor; also father to actor Max Baer Jr., best known as the original Jethro Bodine on *The Beverly Hillbillies*

- **DAVID BECKHAM:** world-class soccer player married to former Spice Girls member Victoria "Posh" Adams, he is Jewish by way of his maternal grandfather and notes in his memoir that he had more direct experience with Judaism growing up than any other religion

- **DANIEL BERGER:** pro golfer by age twenty, ranked twelfth in the PGA in 2020, and hails from tennis champ parents and a golfer grandmother who was inducted into the Greater Buffalo Sports Hall of Fame

- **JOVAN BOOKER:** basketball and soccer star, and adaptive sports community activist who travels across the United States talking about having lost his right leg when he was ten months old due to fibular hemimelia, while fostering athletic organizational opportunities for other amputee athletes

68 As of 2016

- **NATE EBNER:** though he never played in high school, Ebner walked onto his college football team[69] in his junior year, was drafted by the New England Patriots in 2012, earned multiple Super Bowl rings, and became a minority owner in the New England Free Jacks (Major League Rugby)
- **BOBBY FISCHER:** eccentric, outspoken, and controversial grandmaster chess prodigy who won the 1958 US Championship at fourteen, and later became the eleventh-ever World Chess Champion
- **BILL GOLDBERG:** son of a classical violinist father and an award-winning horticulturist mother, he became the only pro wrestler in the sport's history to be WCW World Heavyweight, World Heavyweight, *and* WWE Universal Champion
- **HAILEY ESTHER KOPS:** New York–born pair ice skater who competed as a member of the Israeli team in the 2022 Winter Olympics
- **SANDY KOUFAX:** this left-handed baseball player is considered one of the greatest pitchers the game has ever seen, and, in 1972, became the youngest player elected to the Baseball Hall of Fame
- **NANCY LIEBERMAN:** aka "Lady Magic," this Class of 1999 Women's Basketball Hall of Famer has had one of the most extensive and storied careers in the legacy of the sport, with enduring stints in gameplay, coaching, and as broadcaster

69 The Ohio State Buckeyes

Riverdale, New York City

- Northwestern region of the Bronx, which includes New York City's northernmost point
- Home to a sizable Orthodox Jewish community, the Riverdale Jewish Center, and the Derfner Judaica Museum
- The birthplace of *Ozark*'s multiple-Emmy-winning Jewish actress Julia Garner

Riverdale is "a center for one of New York City's most vibrant Orthodox Jewish communities," as the *New York Times* put it in 1977. The Riverdale Jewish Center alone attracts Jews from at least as far as Stamford, Connecticut . . . such as former US senator and 2000 vice presidential nominee Joe Lieberman. Pretty amazing to think how much Riverdale has grown since the founding of its first synagogue—the Reform Riverdale Temple—as recently as 1947, housed in an abandoned nightclub. Its first Orthodox rabbi was not assigned to the area for another *seven years*, and even then he only had five congregants.

LEARN MORE: According to Christie's International Real Estate, Riverdale's Van Cortlandt Park is even larger than Manhattan's famed Central Park. It may be worth a visit.

Rosenberg, Sol

- Voiced by one-half of the 1990s prank phone call comedy duo the Jerky Boys, Johnny Brennan (aka Johnny B.)
- Known to kvetch to unassuming strangers about his glasses, shoes, and debilitating fear of his shadow choking him

The harrowingly put-upon life of fictional, frantic, fifty-year-old curmudgeon Sol Rosenberg is no joke. So, *why are you laughing*?! He's myopic, oblivious, and frail. He's dangerously accident-prone—be it blowing up his own hand with a firework on the Fourth of July, falling down the stairs, or tripping over his shrieking dog. And, worst of all, he can't ever get anyone he calls to help him . . . particularly as, while he's in mid-jeremiad, they inevitably hang up on him. Rosenberg truly is a caricature in the vein of *South Park*'s Sheila Broflovski, *Futurama*'s Zoidberg, Mike Myers's *Coffee Talk* host Linda Richman on *SNL*,[70] and the entire Saperstein family on *Parks and Recreation*.[71]

> LEARN MORE: Brennan re-created the Rosenberg voice for his role as Jewish pharmacist Mort Goldman on *Family Guy*.

---

70 Based on his Jewish mother-in-law

71 For those who think *The Simpsons*' Professor Frink should be included here, look closely in church scenes where the nerdy inventor can often be spotted in the pews

Rudolph, Maya

- Born July 27, 1972, in Gainesville, Florida
- Became an *SNL* cast member in 2000, exiting in 2007
- Descendant of one of the cofounders of Pittsburgh's Congregation Beth Shalom

Rudolph's career includes impressive roles in films such as *Idiocracy* and *Bridesmaids*, television series such as *The Good Place* and *Big Mouth*, and Emmy Award–winning performances as Kamala Harris on *SNL*. She's also musical, having tickled the keys and sung backup in the Rentals, with whom she recorded the 2004 album *Seven More Minutes*. She later collaborated with Rentals front man Matt Sharp—original bassist for Weezer—and, later still, fellow comedian Triumph the Insult Comic Dog. Perhaps it's a family trait? Her father, Richard Rudolph, is an eclectic songwriter and producer who has collaborated with the likes of Stevie Wonder, the Temptations, Julian Lennon, A Tribe Called Quest, and Tupac Shakur; not to mention his wife and Rudolph's mother, singer Minnie Riperton. In 2001, Rudolph formed her own power couple with filmmaker Paul Thomas Anderson, with whom she has four children.

LEARN MORE: See Rudolph live and in concert, performing with a Prince tribute band, aptly titled Princess.

Seinfeld

- NBC sitcom that first aired on July 5, 1989
- Co-created by Jewish writing partners Larry David and Jerry Seinfeld
- Voted the fifth best television show of all time in a 2015 *Hollywood Reporter* survey of nearly 3,000 prominent industry insiders

WHAT'S the DEAL with Seinfeld? In this famously packaged "show about nothing," Jerry actually only asked "what's the *deal* . . . ?" six times during its nine-season run. The line nevertheless remains a part of its legacy, along with its heir apparent, *Curb Your Enthusiasm*, in which creator Larry David goes on to play a semi-autobiographical version of himself. As disclosed by *TV Guide* in 2014, NBC's then-president and New York–based Jew Brandon Tartikoff nearly nixed *Seinfeld* during development for being "too New York, too Jewish." Fortunately, Tartikoff's successor, Warren Littlefield, championed the show. Littlefield ultimately leveraged *Seinfeld*'s staying power to anchor his "Must See TV"[72] comedy block, dominating the Thursday-night viewership throughout the 1990s.

> LEARN MORE: Jennifer Keishin Armstrong's 2017 *Seinfeldia* tells *all* about, as per its subtitle, "how a show about nothing changed everything."

---

72 Also including the likes of *Frasier, Wings, Mad About You, Friends*, and eventually dramas such as *ER*

Sendak, Maurice

- Born June 10, 1928, in Brooklyn, New York; died May 8, 2012
- Caldecott Medal–winning author of *Where the Wild Things Are* and *In The Night Kitchen*
- Frequent artist partner of fellow Jews, songwriter Carole King and playwright Tony Kushner

Sendak's books have a preternatural ability to make young readers giggle with mischievous glee . . . or quite literally plotz.[73] He found impish delight in monsters, creatures, and animals behaving unnervingly, as well as phantasmagoric dream imagery that borders on the nightmarish. He's known for having proclaimed, "Tell them anything you want!" when it came to creating stories for children. Sendak's legacy represents the possibility that children's books *can* be hilariously mordant, devastatingly grim, wildly jubilant, and beautifully rendered . . . all at once. Sendak lived with his partner, Eugene David Glynn, for fifty years, though Glynn passed away before same-sex marriage was legalized.

> **LEARN MORE:** In addition to Spike Jonze's 2009 Sendak documentary *Tell Them Anything You Want: A Portrait of Maurice Sendak*, there's Kushner's 2003 coffee-table history book *The Art of Maurice Sendak: 1980 to Present*, and 2002's *Last Dance*, a cinema vérité documentary about Sendak's collaboration with a bucolic New Hampshire theater organization.

---

73 Not *quite* what it sounds like . . . but close enough

Seward Park, Seattle

- Became a part of Seattle in 1907
- Represents a three-hundred-acre southeastern section of the city
- Hosts two synagogues—Bikur Holim and Congregation Ezra Bessaroth—that serve Seattle's Sephardim[74]

Dr. Devin Naar, an associate professor who runs a flourishing Sephardic studies program at the University of Washington, described the Seattle area to the *Seattle Times* in 2019 as "a kind of Sephardic hub." After a mass exodus from Seattle's Central District in the 1960s, Seward Park became home to the largest Orthodox Jewish community in the region. As of 2017, 90 percent of the metropolis area's Jews live in Seward Park. And, after Los Angeles and New York, it represents the third-largest Sephardic community nationwide. No wonder Josh Grunig—owner of the Northwest's premier Jewish deli and bakery, Zylberschtein—chose the neighborhood as the ideal locale for his 2022 foodie venture, Muriel's. The eatery serves all manner of homemade Jewish goodies, all supervised by kashruth-observing rabbis . . . some of whom are located elsewhere and power the equipment by remote control. The future is now! *L'chaim!*[75]

LEARN MORE: Out, appropriately enough, through the University of Washington Press in 2003, there's Molly Cone, Howard Droker, and Jacqueline Williams's *Family of Strangers: Building a Jewish Community in Washington State.*

---

74 Jews from the Iberian Peninsula
75 To life!

Shaker Heights, Cleveland

➤ Established as a suburb in 1909, incorporated in 1912
➤ One of the first towns in the region to welcome Black, Catholic, and Jewish residents in the 1950s and 1960s

Cleveland's Jewish population sprouted from its first solo Bavarian immigrant to nearly fifteen hundred who populated the nascent city by the 1860s. By the 1940s, the wealthiest enclave of Cleveland was known as "Yiddishe" or "Jewish Downtown." Prosperous Jews began exiting big city life for eastern suburbs, and the *Cleveland Jewish News* reports that, as of 2022, more than a quarter of the area's one hundred thousand Jews live in what many in the community simply call "the Heights." Notable current and former Jewish residents include: Harlan Ellison, Paul Newman, Harvey Pekar, Susan Orlean, Judith Butler, Joel Grey, Carol Kane, Geraldo Rivera, Roy Lichtenstein, Jerry Siegel, Joe Shuster—and disc jockey Alan Freed, who popularized the term "rock and roll."

LEARN MORE: Shaker Heights is one of the primary locations in Celeste Ng's 2018 bestselling novel *Little Fires Everywhere* and 2003's Shia LaBeouf–starrer *The Battle of Shaker Heights*, a film in which no scene was actually shot on location in Shaker Heights.

Sherman, Allan

- Born Allan Copelon on November 30, 1924
- 1962 debut album *My Son, the Folk Singer* was the fastest-selling record in history at the time
- Sherman's song "Hello Muddah, Hello Fadduh" was inducted into the Library of Congress's National Recording Registry for being "culturally, historically, or aesthetically significant"

While Allan Sherman was one of the original modern song parodists along with peers Stan Freberg and Tom Lehrer, his status as a memorable iconoclast still resonates today. Just ask Homer Simpson, who knocked "Weird Al" Yankovic down a peg after the accordion-playing parody king suggested two songs Homer had sent him sounded the same. "Yeah, like you and Allan Sherman," was Homer's witty rejoinder. The sui generis voice that briefly made Sherman a star throughout the 1960s can also be heard in the original *Cat in the Hat* cartoons. Sherman's the Cat.

LEARN MORE: For insight into the man, in his own words, there's Sherman's autobiography, 1965's *A Gift of Laughter.*

Shtetl

- *Haimish* market villages in Eastern Europe where Jews were cordoned off from gentile countrymen prior to the Holocaust
- Diminutive of the Yiddish *shtot*, or "large city"
- Recently redefined by Distinguished Professor of Jewish Studies at Rutgers University Jeffrey Shandler to mean *any* "little town"

If you've seen *Fiddler on the Roof*, you've seen a shtetl. There's also the shtetl in which the primary action takes place in Jonathan Safran Foer's *Everything Is Illuminated*, whose film adaptation starred Elijah Wood and Gogol Bordello front man Eugene Hütz. Simon Rich's short story "Sell Out" was adapted into the 2020 Seth Rogen–starrer *An American Pickle*, which once again presents a fairly accurate depiction of an early twentieth-century shtetl. Speaking of pickled vegetables, it's worth noshing on the fact that preferred foods in shtetls tended toward rye bread and sauerkraut, heavy in probiotics and thus a fine nutrient shield from common diseases of the time.

> **LEARN MORE:** Ukrainian scholar of Soviet Yiddish history and literature Gennady Estraikh has proclaimed it a historical disservice to exclude the large number of *non*-Jewish shtetl residents in his book, *The Shtetl: Image and Reality*. You can also feast your eyes on radiant renderings of the little villages in the paintings of former shtetl resident Marc Chagall.

Sitka, Alaska (fictional)

- Although there is an actual Sitka, this entry is a *hatze-platz*[76] that solely exists in the 2007 novel *The Yiddish Policemen's Union*
- The novel was written by Pulitzer Prize–winning Jewish author Michael Chabon

In Chabon's award-winning sci-fi detective novel, Sitka became a sprawling Jewish hub during World War II after the US government followed through with setting aside a parcel of Alaska for Holocaust-fleeing European Jews, as recommended by the 1940 Slattery Report. In reality, the report *did* indeed exist . . . but was squelched even before it could be voted on. Through the magic of Chabon's rewriting of historical events, Sitka's existence saved the lives of four million Jews who secured safe haven in the southeast Alaskan settlement. With so many people living in such a small area, it's no wonder that this Sitka evokes a Jewish *Blade Runner*–esque noir setting, lined with an underbelly of crime, drugs, and gangs. A tough place to live, sure—but some of the best pastrami sandwiches this side of the Arctic.

> LEARN MORE: In addition to reading Chabon's novel, you can also check into the Jewish Alaskan adventures of fish-out-of-water Dr. Joel Fleischman in the hit 1990s show *Northern Exposure.*

---

76 Proverbial faraway place, as in "way the heck out in *hatzeplatz!*"

South Africa

- Officially known as the Republic of South Africa (RSA)
- The twenty-third most populated nation worldwide, with sixty million residents
- The 52,000 Jews who call South Africa home represent the largest Jewish community on the continent and the eleventh largest globally[77]

The first Jews to arrive in South Africa, in the 1480s, were cartographers employed by the Portuguese Crown to seek out a potential ocean route to India. But it wasn't until the 1820s that Jews began to more densely populate the area, and then mostly in Cape Town. In this one of three capital cities the first South African synagogue, Cape Town Hebrew Congregation, was founded on the eve of Yom Kippur in 1841. It was initially part of a house owned by a Jew who had settled in the country two decades earlier. Today, it's nestled within the Cape Town Botanical Gardens and has taken on the apropos name of the Gardens Shul.

LEARN MORE: Take a trip through Tzippi Hoffman and Alan Fischer's 1988 book *The Jews of South Africa: What Future?* or stop on over to Richard Mendelsohn and Milton Shain's 2009 *The Jews in South Africa: An Illustrated History.*

---

77 As of September 2021

South Florida

- Encompassing Fort Lauderdale, the Florida Keys, the Miami metropolitan area, Boca Raton, Boynton Beach, and West Palm Beach
- The state of Florida boasts the seventh-largest Jewish population per capita in the country[78]
- Is the southernmost region of the continental United States

This was where many Jews first arrived in America (sometimes literally *shipwrecked*) after escaping European persecution in the 1880s. However, in the early 1980s, "you couldn't even get a decent bagel in this county," according to Bill Gralnick, Southeast regional director of the American Jewish Committee, in a 2005 *Palm Beach Post* interview. But by April 2022, the Jewish publication *Mosaic* reported that "South Florida emerged as a vital hub of Jewish life. Bringing together Latin Jews, Orthodox Jews, secular Israelis, and Jewish migrants from the northeast, the region has nourished a distinctively American Jewish culture unlike anywhere else in the world."

> LEARN MORE: Zeroing in on Jewish retirees in the Miami area, the 2018 documentary *The Last Resort* premiered at the Miami Jewish Film Festival, where it won the Audience Award for Best Documentary . . . before being screened next at the Palm Beach Jewish Film Festival.

78 As of 2022

Stamford Hill, England

- Northeast London hamlet with recorded name variations dating back to the thirteenth century
- Both a railway and tram came in 1872, transforming the rural area into a bustling interchange for London area travelers
- Known as "the square mile of piety," it is home to the largest concentration of Haredi[79] Jews in Europe

In addition to its Hasidic community that first arrived in the 1920s, Stamford Hill is populated by Yemenite Jews, many of whom fled to the region in the 1960s to escape nationwide political turmoil in their native country. The close-knit interconnectivity of Jews in the area greatly assisted Stamford Hill's ability to cope during the rise of COVID-19. "Not on my fingers and toes could I count the times I've been helped by community organizations recently," convalescing elder Stamford Hill resident Eli Sufrin told *The Guardian* in May 2020—a peak time for the pandemic.

> **LEARN MORE:** Documentary photographer Andrew Aitchison spent five years living and working with the Haredi Jews of Stamford Hill and captured this experience in his 2009 book *Orthodox Jewish Life*.

79 Strict Orthodox; of which Hasidic Jews are a subsect

Stern

- Authored by Bruce Jay Friedman (1930–2020)
- Published by Simon & Schuster in 1962
- Regarded as the first "Freudian novel"

Bruce Jay Friedman's wry, sardonic wit was so revolutionary and influential, it endures through the legacy of the comedy style he popularized: "black humor."[80] As per the 1965 collection of short stories so titled that he edited—which included such like-minded contributors as Thomas Pynchon, Terry Southern, and Vladimir Nabokov—Friedman was an indisputable master of a tone at once cartoonish *and* deadpan, apoplectic *and* feckless, obscene *and* penitent. Nowhere was this tightrope walk as masterfully clinched than in his first novel, *Stern*, a darkly comic, absurdly paranoiac, and devastatingly incisive story about the "modern-day" frustrations of reconciling being both a Jewish mensch and an "average Joe" in stagnant mid-twentieth-century America.

> LEARN MORE: Friedman turned his indolent and biting humor in on himself in his intimately candid memoir, *Lucky Bruce*. As he writes, it was after *Stern* that he decided to "Take the money, scribble a bit, and enjoy the room service" as a hitmaking writer of such films as *Splash* and *Stir Crazy*.

---

80 Comedy that lampoons very serious things, such as death

Streisand, Barbra

- Born April 24, 1942, in Brooklyn, New York
- Only person to have had a *Billboard*-topping album in each of the past six decades
- *And* the only person to have earned an Oscar, Tony, Emmy, Grammy, Golden Globe, CableACE, and Peabody Award

Barbra Streisand survived a childhood being bullied for her singular style and implacable ambition. This included a challenging relationship with her mother, and the loss of her father who passed away when she was fifteen months old. Yet she forged headlong into a successful singing career that led to her 1968 breakout portrayal of *Funny Girl*'s iconic Jewish singer-comedian Fanny Brice. Streisand has gone on to embrace both her heritage and remarkable performance range, directing and starring in the heart-wrenching musical *Yentl*, and playing a comedically quintessential Jewish mother in both *Meet the Fockers* and *The Guilt Trip*.

LEARN MORE: Streisand has yet to release her long-awaited autobiography. So, those wanting to know the full inside tale of the little lady with the voluminous voice will have to settle for the 2017 performance tour documentary *Barbra: The Music... The Mem'ries... The Magic!* For now.

Sufganiyot

- Round, deep-fried but pillowy dough filled with custard or jelly and dusted by a gentle flurry of powdered sugar
- A staple of the Chanukah menu, with the oil in which it's fried representing the eight nights of light produced from a limited reserve of lamp oil

First, there were jelly doughnuts in fifteenth-century Europe. By the nineteenth century, they were called "Berliners" in—you guessed it—*Germany*. Polish Jews then tweaked the recipe by using schmaltz or oil in lieu of lard to keep kosher the food that they would ultimately call a *ponchik*. When some of these Polish Jews made their way to what would become present-day Israel, their *ponchik* was renamed after the Talmudic words for "sponge" (*sofgan*) and "dough" (*sfogga*). And, there you have it: your mouthwatering *sufganiyah*.

LEARN MORE: Delve into this decadent delicacy with an expert of intermingling Ashkenazic and Sephardic Jewish culinary traditions, Miriam Gurov, who instructs in the ways of the kashruth arts at Jerusalem's Nativ Institute, and in 2020 published *Sufganiyot, Latkes and More Hanukkah Traditional Foods: 20 Easy & Delicious Israeli Recipes.*

Superhero Origin Stories

Whether it's the founder of Comic-Con Shel Dorf, *Wonder Woman* actress Gal Gadot, illustrative innovator Rube Goldberg, or even *characters* like *Fantastic Four*'s the Thing, there's plenty of Jewish representation in the comics scene. Here are a few high-flying heroes of the medium:

- **ROZ CHAST:** renowned staff cartoonist for the *New Yorker* who has produced thousands of thoughtful, sardonic illustrations in her signature playfully minimalist style since 1978
- **ENID COLESLAW**[81]**:** snarky proto-emo protagonist of mid-'90s comic series, graphic novel, and film adaptation *Ghost World*
- **WILL EISNER:** there's good reason that the Oscars of comic books are named "the Eisners": he is considered the father of graphic novels, his 1940 flagship series *The Spirit* still holds influential sway throughout the industry today, and as seminal comics creator Frank Miller proclaimed: "If there were a Mount Rushmore of comics, Will Eisner would be George Washington"
- **ALINE KOMINSKY-CRUMB:** early underground comix creator who pioneered a ruthlessly confessional style, Aline was a forerunner of injecting feminism into comics, coediting multiple editions of the all-women comics anthology *Twisted Sisters* for two decades

81 An anagram of Jewish creator Daniel Clowes's name

- **STAN LEE AND JACK KIRBY:** dynamic duo behind Marvel Comics, outrageously charismatic visionary Lee (né Lieber) did a lot of the "talkin'" while the buttoned-down workhorse Kirby did a lot of the "walkin'"
- **MAGNETO:** this powerful mutant reigns supreme over the adversarial elements of Marvel's *X-Men*-verse, while at the same time being compared to various civil rights leaders for his by-any-means-necessary approach to violent injustice against his fellow mutants
- **HARLEY QUINN:** henchwoman, sometimes life partner, and former mild-mannered psychiatrist of Batman's archnemesis the Joker
- **JERRY SIEGEL AND JOE SHUSTER:** boyhood pals who created one of the first and most recognizable superheroes of all time—Superman
- **LEN WEIN:** co-creator of iconic characters Wolverine, Swamp Thing, Nightcrawler, Storm, Colossus, and Lucius Fox; and editor of Alan Moore's highly acclaimed *Watchmen*

Talking It Out

The gift of gab is strong in *This American Life*'s Ira Glass, *WTF*'s Marc Maron, television personality Maury Povich, and these fellow kibitzers:

- **WOLF BLITZER:** an integral fixture of CNN, hosting his own show *The Situation Room with Wolf Blitzer* for the past two decades
- **DR. JOYCE BROTHERS:** psychologist who rose to fame by winning *The $64,000 Question*, after which she hosted *Living Easy with Dr. Joyce Brothers*
- **DR. DREW:** David Drew Pinsky has dedicated his career to assisting patients struggling with chemical dependency and addiction, eventually hosting his own series—*Loveline*
- **LARRY KING:** one of the most recognizable talk show hosts of all time, conducted more than fifty thousand interviews throughout an eclectic seven-decade-long career
- **SALLY JESSY RAPHAEL:** as a teenager, Sally Lowenthal read the news for her local radio station before adopting the moniker that lasted her nearly two decades as host of *The Sally Jessy Raphael Show*
- **JOAN RIVERS:** fearlessly brash comedian and regular guest host on *The Tonight Show Starring Johnny Carson* before hosting the first-ever FOX series, *The Late Show Starring Joan Rivers*, and thereafter becoming a formidable on-screen fashionista and celebrity quidnunc

- **HOWARD STERN:** provocative talk radio host of the eponymous *Howard Stern Show* and judge on *America's Got Talent*
- **JON STEWART:** a comedian who bounced around MTV and Comedy Central before regularly playing a version of himself on *The Larry Sanders Show*: an uncannily prescient series that includes an episode in which the characters contend with a network owner's suggestion that they need a new kind of late-night news program with a hip MTV sensibility AND ends with Stewart's character replacing Sanders . . . eight years before the *actual* Stewart became the host of *The Daily Show*
- **MIKE WALLACE:** this esteemed journalist, actor, and author is probably best known as the centerpiece and original cohost of *60 Minutes*
- **DR. RUTH WESTHEIMER:** Karola Ruth Westheimer spent her youth in a Switzerland orphanage as an escapee from the Holocaust, before studying psychology at the Sorbonne, immigrating to the United States, and finding her niche as a renowned sex therapist and radio/television host

Tel Aviv

- Founded April 11, 1909, as a Jewish suburb of what was at the time Jaffa
- Known as Israel's cosmopolitan tech/financial hub

The name comes from Zionism founder Theodor Herzl's 1902 utopian novel *Altneuland*,[82] which pioneering Hebrew journalist Nahum Sokolow translated into Hebrew as Tel Aviv.[83] It may also be historically connected to Tel-abib, a possibly mythological section of Babylon, now in present-day Iraq, that the Book of Ezekiel chronicles as being an early ghetto for Jews forcefully exiled from places nearby. Today, Tel Aviv is globally recognized for culinary delights, entertainment extravaganzas, and unique tourist attractions. An UNESCO World Heritage Site, Tel Aviv is home to the country's largest international airport, biggest university, and tallest skyscrapers.

> **LEARN MORE:** TLV1 is an English-language podcast network based in Tel Aviv; its programs focus on all elements of living in the city.

82 German for "The Old New Land"
83 "Tell" (mound) of "barley ripening" (spring)

The Three Stooges

- On-screen innovators of the physical comedy form known as "slapstick"
- Their original run was from 1922 to 1970
- Earned a collective Hollywood Walk of Fame star in 1983

The Stooges' most recognizable members included: Moe Howard (Moses Harry Horwitz), Larry Fine (Louis Feinberg), and Curly Howard (Jerome Lester Horwitz). Though first, they were the vaudevillian performers known as "Ted Healy and His Stooges," in which Moe, Larry, and Shemp (Moses's brother Samuel) played intentionally irritating comedic relief to founder and star Healy. Then they tried their hand on celluloid with 1930's feature-length *Soup to Nuts*, where they stood out enough to be offered a deal by the production studio in charge, Fox. One catch: Healy wasn't invited along. Hollywood business shenanigans ensued, Healy was able to stymie the Stooges' move forward, and the Healy-less troupe had to go out into showbiz wilderness alone. Luckily, the Three Stooges did so quite productively for decades on film and TV, in cartoons, comic books, video games . . . and just about everywhere and anywhere else someone could throw a pie or get whacked (*loudly*) by a hammer on the head.

> **LEARN MORE:** Teach the children well . . . and read to them from Pam Pollack and Meg Belviso's *Who Were the Three Stooges?*, illustrated by Ted Hammond.

Tikva Records

➤ Active from 1947 to the late 1970s
➤ Produced nearly two hundred albums and audiobooks

According to vinyl historian and USC associate professor Josh Kun, the independent record label's lasting legacy was as "a veritable grab-bag of American-Jewish identities and styles from the years following WWII." Even so, founder and operator Allen B. Jacobs was no match for contemporaries Leonard and Phil Chess, Jewish immigrant brothers whose legendary label[84] helped launch the blues and R&B scene a decade before Motown. Jacobs, meanwhile, destroyed all his "budget" label's album masters during a deal gone awry. Featured Tikva Records artists included Martha Schlamme, whose repertoire ranged from an album with then-blacklisted Pete Seeger to songs composed by classical maestro Kurt Weill; Polish-born Holocaust survivor Tova Ben Zvi, who specializes in Yiddish songs; and Lazarus "Leo" Fuld who, at eighty-three, recorded his final album that impresario Abe Goldstein called "the *Sgt. Pepper* of Yiddish music."

LEARN MORE: Professor Kun and fellow enthusiasts formed the nonprofit, volunteer-based Idelsohn Society for Musical Preservation, which put out the 2011 Tikva Records omnibus, *Songs of the Jewish-American Jet Set*.

---

84 Which recorded the likes of Howlin' Wolf, Bo Diddley, Muddy Waters, Buddy Guy, and Chuck Berry

Tzedakah

- Hebrew word for "righteousness"
- Emphasizes contributions of time, energy, and wise counsel, over financial offerings
- The phrase "natan" (Hebrew for "to give") is a purposeful palindrome, believed to suggest that donor and recipient should work in reciprocal tandem

Tzedakah, one of the most important mitzvoth (good deeds)[85] in Jewish culture, refers to the ethical obligation to work toward social justice, particularly by means of philanthropic gestures. Observant Jews may have in their synagogues or households blue-and-white *pushkas*—contribution boxes made from tin into which alms can be deposited—or fur pouches for that same purpose. Though there are various tiers of suggested tzedakah depending on the available resources of the contributor, it is today typical of religious Jews to donate 10 percent of their annual income as part of a specific act of the tradition known as *ma'sar kesafim*.

> LEARN MORE: Volunteer at your local soup kitchen or to babysit your neighbor's kids. Give a 50 percent tip at your favorite restaurant. Mazel tov: you'll be learning about (and taking part in) the joys of tzedakah.

85 One of 613 Jewish commandments

Vaudeville

- First developed in late nineteenth-century France as a form of egalitarian variety show to amuse the middle class
- Referred to in the aptly titled 2006 book *No Applause— Just Throw Money* as "the heart of American show business" for decades (1881–1932, to be exact)
- A means for immigrants in the United States to ascend the ranks of the cultural and financial echelon

Before there was *American Idol*, before there was Hollywood . . . there was vaudeville. And if you aspired to perform on its remorseless traveling carnivalesque circuit, you'd better be good. At *everything*. You better be able to play the violin. You better be able to sing. Perform magic. Conduct a pack of trained seals honking bike horns. You better be able to make 'em laugh. Otherwise? You wouldn't make enough money to eat that week. Or maybe they'd throw vegetables at you. Maybe *worse*. But if you *were* good, you could become a *star*. Just ask such legendary *badkhonim*[86] as: Harry Houdini, Sophie Tucker, the Marx Bros., Fanny Brice, Eddie Cantor, and Al Jolson.

> **LEARN MORE:** Though Charlie Chaplin wasn't Jewish, his half-brother *Sydney* was, and you can watch the story of how vaudeville changed Charlie's life—along with the entirety of modern entertainment as we know it—in Richard Attenborough's masterful 1992 film *Chaplin*.

---

86 Jewish entertainers, typically clowns/jesters for celebrations such as weddings

Yeshiva

- Instruction is largely conducted through oral, Socratic tradition
- Emphasizes two cornerstone texts of rabbinical study: the Torah (Jewish law/instruction) and Talmud (commentary on/interpretation of Torah)
- Mir Yeshiva, aka "The Mir," is the largest of its kind in the world, with an enrollment of nearly 10,000 rabbinical students

So, you want to be a rabbi. This means you may want to attend a yeshiva. Once there, you'll be immersed in an extremely rigorous environment, taught by way of conventional lectures known as *shiurim*, supplemented with *chavrusas* (intensive debates between two study partners). In yeshiva, a student is called a *ben Torah* who adheres to *halacha* or "behavioral laws" in order to become wholly pious, receive *smicha*,[87] and—*boom*—exit as an officiated rabbi.

LEARN MORE: Based on Isaac Bashevis Singer's short-story-turned-play, the Barbra Streisand film *Yentl* centers on a female protagonist who, prior to yeshiva becoming coed in the 1940s, defies tradition to present as a boy who wants to become a *ben Torah*. All while maintaining perfect pitch throughout a spectacularly produced songbook.

87 Ordination

You Oughta Be in Pictures

Jews have played an indelible role in cinema, from the days of the early studio moguls to such popular modern-day mavens as Steven Spielberg and the Coen Bros. Here's further B-roll of those who have made a career out of three magical words: "Lights, camera, action!"

- **HÉCTOR BABENCO:** Argentine-Brazilian writer-director who produced *Kiss of the Spider Woman*, Jack Nicholson/Meryl Streep–starrer *Ironweed*, and *Pixote*—crucially inspirational to the indie filmmaking crowd of the 1990s, especially Jewish enfant terrible Harmony Korine

- **ALBERT BROOKS:** shining star both in front of and behind the camera, whose comedies include such thoughtful laugh riots as *Lost in America*, *Modern Romance*, and *Defending Your Life*

- **ANDREW BUJALSKI:** writer-director considered the godfather of mumblecore—an uber-DIY indie movement of early 2000s cinema and generative launchpad for Greta Gerwig, Lynn Shelton, Joe Swanberg, the Duplass Bros., Lena Dunham, David Lowery, and Alex Ross Perry

- **SERGEI EISENSTEIN:** Soviet moviemaker and theorist who first utilized the montage, devised by Eisenstein's mentor, Lev Kuleshov, as exemplified in the 1925 film *Battleship Potemkin*

- **NORA EPHRON:** Academy Award–winning screenwriter who reinvented the modern rom-com with such films as

When Harry Met Sally . . . (directed by fellow Jew Rob
Reiner), *Sleepless in Seattle*, and *You've Got Mail*

➤ **MAX FLEISCHER:** early animation trendsetter who
conjured enduring characters Betty Boop and Popeye, and
spearheaded such on-screen wizardry as rotoscoping,[88]
the "bouncing ball" technique for song lyrics, and the
stereoptical process[89]

➤ **HERSCHELL GORDON LEWIS:** "Godfather of Gore"
who concocted the genre aptly called "splatter" due to
its overabundance of colorful viscera for use in imp-
ishly twisted sequences that intentionally elicit as much
gut-wrenching laughter as surrealistic horror

➤ **ERROL MORRIS:** pioneered new forms of nonfiction
storytelling and technological innovations alike, including
in 1988's *The Thin Blue Line*, which is widely revered as
one of the best documentaries ever made

➤ **JULIE TAYMOR:** made her historical mark with 1997's
The Lion King stage production, as well as with such
highly lauded films as: *Titus*, *Across the Universe*, and the
stylistic biopics on artist Frida Kahlo and feminist leader
Gloria Steinem

➤ **BILLY WILDER:** outrageously prolific and uncannily
versatile filmmaker nominated for twenty-one Academy
Awards (winning six), responsible for: *Double Indemnity*,
The Seven Year Itch, *Some Like It Hot*, and *Sunset Boulevard*

---

88 Using live-action scenes as the rubric for drawing
89 Means of making more distinct the foreground and background elements so as to
create the illusion of three dimensions of movement on-screen

A FINAL WORD AND ZEI GEZUNT![90]

There's a charmingly memorable moment in the 1996 sci-fi/action extravaganza *Independence Day*. The father of Jeff Goldblum's character, played by Judd Hirsch,[91] is holding a prayer vigil in Hebrew. Another character, when invited to join in, dowdily confesses that he's not Jewish. To which Hirsch's character responds, "Nobody's perfect."

What I love best about this moment is that the punch line reflects the idea that Jewish culture is based on forever exploring, questioning, and critiquing the very *idea* of "perfection."

It's built into the *foundation* of Judaism that we are constantly seeking future possibilities ahead. We are dissatisfied with what things are *now*, and are in the constant throes of wondering and wandering in search of *whatever's next*. In essence, what may be "perfect" today . . . could very likely prove to be quite *im*perfect tomorrow. *So, let's keep pressing onward.*

That's a lot of what this book is about: bringing together many Jewish innovators, pioneers, thinkers, and wanderers for whom "perfection" is merely subjective and in constant flux. This is why they were or are so often changing, evolving, growing, and doing what they could and can to instill a sense of constant progression in the lives of those around them.

"Perfection" itself may be merely illusory. But, acknowledging and remembering and discussing those who aspired to it? That's something well worth a read. *We hope.*

---

90 "Be well!"
91 Both Goldblum and Hirsch are Jewish, by the by

RESOURCES

Can We Talk? is a podcast produced by the JWA (Jewish Women's Archive) that brings together discussions and analyses of topics pertinent to Jewish women

An Empire of Their Own: How the Jews Invented Hollywood, by Neal Gabler, is a deep-dive account of the first Jewish immigrants to discover and redefine American cinema

Encyclopedia of Jewish Food, by Gil Marks, is an extensive guidebook for readers interested in both a variety of Jewish foodie recipes *and* the history behind them

Jewish Telegraphic Agency, jta.org, was founded in 1917 and is a not-for-profit international news network run by an independent board that serves the global Jewish community

Jewish Virtual Library, jewishvirtuallibrary.org, is a comprehensive online database of more than twenty-five thousand entries about Jewish history, serving nearly one million unique visitors a month

Old Jews Telling Jokes, established in 2008 by Sam Hoffman, is a web series, book, and traveling performance showcase through which—*yup!*—old Jews tell lengthy jokes

Unorthodox, hosted by Mark Oppenheimer, Stephanie Butnick, and Liel Leibovitz, is a weekly podcast produced by *Tablet* focusing on topical issues in the Jewish community

The Wandering Muse, by Tamás Wormser, is a 2014 feature-length documentary exploring worldwide Jewish identity through music

REFERENCES

Aroesty, Sophie. "It's Going to Be a 'Wet Hot' Summer. Again!" *Tablet*, June 26, 2017. tabletmag.com/sections/news/articles/its-going-to-be-a-wet-hot-summer-again.

Auld, Tim, et al. "The 50 Greatest Food Stores in the World." *Financial Times*, May 18, 2021. ft.com/content/684252ce-7b37-4a2a-a0f7-15fe19e071d9.

Browne, David. "Goldie and the Gingerbreads Were One of Rock's First All-Women Bands. Why Are They Still So Obscure?" *Rolling Stone*, July 1, 2021. rollingstone.com/music/music-features/goldie-gingerbreads-interview-genya-ravan-1187909.

Cohen, Bennett, and Jerry Greenfield. "We're Ben and Jerry. Men of Ice Cream, Men of Principle." *New York Times*, July 28, 2021. nytimes.com/2021/07/28/opinion/ben-and-jerry-israel.html.

Cooperman, Jeannette. "Confessions of a Hydrox Cookie." *The Common Reader*, January 9, 2022. commonreader.wustl.edu/confessions-of-a-hydrox-cookie.

Crowley, Chris E. "Inside New York's Cult of the Bialy." *Serious Eats*, August 10, 2018. seriouseats.com/bialy-new-york-bread.

Elliott, Stuart. "Humor and a 'Higher Authority' Help Spice Up a New Campaign for Hebrew National." *New York Times*, May 23, 1997. nytimes.com/1997/05/23/business/humor-higher-authority-help-spice-up-new-campaign-for-hebrew-national-franks.html.

Greer, Germaine. "The Betty I Knew." *The Guardian*, February 7, 2006. theguardian.com/world/2006/feb/07/gender.bookscomment.

Hester, Jessica Leigh. "'Man, Oh Manischewitz': When the Jewish Wine Was Big with Gentiles, Too." NPR, April 22, 2016. npr.org/sections/thesalt/2016/04/22/475142479/man-oh-manichewitz-when-the-jewish-wine-was-big-with-gentiles-too.

Hutton, Grey. "How a Haredi Community in London Is Coping with Coronavirus." *The Guardian*, May 26, 2020. theguardian.com/world/2020/may/26/how-a-haredi-community-in-london-is-coping-with-coronavirus-photo-essay.

Ingall, Marjorie. "Introducing: The Greatest Children's Book Ever Written About Gefilte Fish." *Tablet,* June 20, 2018. tabletmag.com/sections/news/articles/introducing-the-greatest-childrens-book-ever-written-about-gefilte-fish.

The Kitchen Sisters. "Give Chickpeas a Chance: Why Hummus Unites, and Divides, the Mideast." NPR, July 18, 2016. npr.org/sections/thesalt/2016/07/18/483715410/give-chickpeas-a-chance-why-hummus-unites-and-divides-the-mideast.

KosherToday. "Major NYC Hospital Reshuffles Kosher Program." *KosherToday,* December 14, 2015. koshertoday.com/news/major-nyc-hospital-reshuffles-kosher-program.

LaBorde, Monique. "A Fishing Line Encircles Manhattan, Protecting Sanctity of Sabbath." NPR, May 13, 2019. npr.org/2019/05/13/721551785/a-fishing-line-encircles-manhattan-protecting-sanctity-of-sabbath.

MacFarquhar, Neil. "At the New Year, a New Day for Riverdale; A Bronx Neighborhood Is Now a Lively Center for Orthodox Jews." *New York Times*, October 1, 1997. nytimes.com/1997/10/01/nyregion/new-year-new-day-for-riverdale-bronx-neighborhood-now-lively-center-for-orthodox.html.

Masunaga, Samantha. "How I Made It: Norm Langer Guides Langer's Deli through Changing Tastes." *Los Angeles Times*, April 14, 2018. latimes.com/business/la-fi-himi-langer-20180414-htmlstory.html.

Montagne, Renee. "Itzhak Perlman: I'm Not on the Stage to Walk, I'm on It to Play." NPR, November 27, 2015. npr.org/2015/11/27/457419476/itzhak-perlman-im-not-on-the-stage-to-walk-im-on-it-to-play.

Nathan, Joan. "On Hanukkah, the Latke Road Less Traveled." *New York Times*, December 1, 2015. nytimes.com/2015/12/02/dining/latkes-mashed-potatoes-recipe.html.

NPR. "Reviving 'Songs for the Jewish-American Jet Set.'" NPR, December 15, 2011. npr.org/2011/12/15/143771771/reviving-songs-for-the-jewish-american-jet-set.

Olmsted, Larry. "Katz's Delicatessen in New York: Is America's Most Famous Jewish Deli Worth a Trip?" *USA Today*, March 14, 2019. usatoday.com/story/travel/columnist/greatamericanbites/2019/03/14/katz-deli-new-york-city/3155601002.

Oringel, Amy. "Brooklyn's Joyva Has a Helluva Halvah Story." *The Forward*, January 21, 2018. forward.com/culture/392201/brooklyns-joyva-has-a-helluva-halvah-story.

Paul, Larisha. "Tiffany Haddish Announces New Essay Collection 'I Curse You with Joy.'" *Rolling Stone*, March 25, 2022. rollingstone.com/culture/culture-news/tiffany-haddish -essay-collection-i-curse-you-with-joy-1326783.

Peiser, Jaclyn. "Anti-Semitism's Rise Gives *The Forward* New Resolve." *New York Times*, October 8, 2017. nytimes.com/2017/ 10/08/business/media/the-forward-antisemitism.html.

Prochnik, George. "A Guide to Religious Anarchy: Gershom Scholem's Kabbalah." *New Yorker*, March 14, 2017. newyorker .com/books/page-turner/a-guide-to-religious-anarchy-gershom -scholems-kabbalah.

Raab, Scott. "My Blintz with Paul Giamatti." *Esquire*, November 19, 2007. esquire.com/entertainment/movies/a3878/giamatti1207.

Raspe, Becky. "A Look at Jewish Cleveland's Past, Present, Future." *Cleveland Jewish News*, May 1, 2022. clevelandjewishnews.com/ news/jpro/a-look-at-jewish-cleveland-s-past-present-future/ article_54ddc6e0-c72f-11ec-b233-4bd03ee3537e.html.

Sernovitz, Gary. "I Do Not Want to Dance the Hora." *Slate*, June 29, 2012. slate.com/human-interest/2012/06/hora-and -my-jewish-wedding-forget-tradition-i-will-not-dance.html.

Shapiro, Nina. "Jews from around the World Come to Seattle to See the U.S.' 3rd Largest Sephardic Community." *Seattle Times*, May 29, 2019. seattletimes.com/seattle-news/jews-from-around -the-world-come-to-seattle-to-see-the-u-s-3rd-largest-sephardic -community.

Swartz, Tracy. "How Rachel Brosnahan's Highland Park Roots Influenced Her 'Mrs. Maisel' Role." *Chicago Tribune*, November 27, 2017. chicagotribune.com/entertainment/ct-ent-rachel-brosnahan-marvelous-mrs-maisel-20171127-story.html.

Traves, Lindsay. "The Jewish Origins of the Vulcan Salute." *The Canadian Jewish News*, September 22, 2021. thecjn.ca/arts/the-jewish-origins-of-the-vulcan-salute.

Yakas, Ben. "'Too New York, Too Jewish:' The 30th Anniversary of 'The Seinfeld Chronicles' Pilot." *Gothamist*, July 5, 2019. gothamist.com/arts-entertainment/too-new-york-too-jewish-the-30th-anniversary-of-the-seinfeld-chronicles-pilot.

Zimmer, Ben. "A History of *Meh*, from Leo Rosten to Auden to *The Simpsons*." *Slate*, September 6, 2013. slate.com/human-interest/2013/09/meh-etymology-tracing-the-yiddish-word-from-leo-rosten-to-auden-to-the-simpsons.html.

INDEX

Acknowledgments

Thanks, as always, to the author's incredibly supportive friends and family who continue to encourage his constant creative conjuring and stubbornly independent lifestyle.

Gratitude to Bill Bryson, whose 2010 book *At Home* lent much inspiration to the penning of *The Little Encyclopedia of Jewish Culture*. So, too, the music of Charlie Parker, Glenn Gould, Joe Albany, Lead Belly, and Radiohead.

The author additionally recognizes and thanks Salmon Taymuree and the team at his publisher for inviting him along this journey. This includes in no short measure Leila Sales and the author's primary editor, Alexis Sattler, who represents all of the best elements of what a book editor can and should be.

And, of course, to Becky—the Alma Elson to his Reynolds Woodcock.

About the Author

Mathew Klickstein is a longtime writer, producer, and instructor whose reportage has appeared in such outlets as *WIRED*, the *New York Daily News*, and *Vulture*, and whose twenty books to date predominantly focus on extensive, firsthand pop culture histories, including those of *The Simpsons*, Comic-Con, and the Nickelodeon network. He is also the screenwriter of Sony Pictures' *Against the Dark*, creator of AfterShock's highly acclaimed comic book series *You Are Obsolete*, and creator of the SiriusXM/Stitcher documentary podcast series *Comic-Con Begins*, available free on all audio platforms. He lives in Dayton, Ohio, with his wife, Becky, and their dog Adjunct Professor David Foster Wallace. His website is mathewklickstein.com.